Abraham Lincoln
and the
End of Slavery
in the
District of Columbia

Capitol Hill in 1851. Lincoln's boarding house is in Square 729, the bowling alley where he bowled in Square 688. Lincoln Park (unnamed at the time) is due east of the Capitol at the right edge of this detail. The Navy Yard is at the middle of the bottom of the map. For more information on Lincoln's Capitol Hill, see p. 17.

Detail of map published by Lloyd Van Derveer, Camden, N.J. (from Library of Congress)

To Laure
Thanks for reading

Abraham Lincoln

and the

End of Slavery

in the

District of Columbia

Edited by Robert S. Pohl
and John R. Wennersten

Eastern Branch Press · Washington
2009

ISBN: 978-0-578-01688-7

Manufactured in the United States of America

First Edition

FOREWORD

To mark the bicentennial of Abraham Lincoln's birth, Friends of Southeast Library offers this account of Lincoln and our neighborhood.

Capitol Hill includes many highly visible links to the nation's sixteenth president, including Lincoln Park, along with Stanton Park and Seward Square, named for two players on the "team of rivals" that served in Abraham Lincoln's cabinet.

Lincoln's legacy endures as the president who preserved the Union and removed the stigma of slavery that so divided a new nation founded on the concept of freedom for all. And it is our neighborhood's connection to that story that this book recounts—the story of abolition, emancipation and celebration that fulfilled the promise envisioned by the Founders.

Our major focus is the relatively unknown history of the first freed, the slaves in the District of Columbia, where freedom came on April 16, 1862—nine months before Lincoln issued the Emancipation Proclamation and almost three years before the Thirteenth Amendment to the Constitution extended freedom to slaves throughout the country.

Lincoln had proposed freeing the slaves in D.C. when he first came to Capitol Hill in 1847 as a Member of Congress. As a freshman legislator, he challenged President James K. Polk on the Mexican War, introducing the "spot resolutions," demanding to know the precise spot on which Mexicans had shed American blood. The war debates opened the most serious question before the 30th Congress—whether the newly won territories should allow slavery—and Lincoln's eyes were opened to the explosiveness and divisiveness of the slavery question on the national political stage.

Lincoln observed slavery's brutality and violence, and he described seeing a slave market near the Capitol, "where Negroes were collected, temporarily kept, and finally taken to Southern markets, precisely like droves of horses."

After a single term in the House, Lincoln returned to Illinois, emerging as the Republican Party nominee for president and winning the 1860 election.

Spoken October 16, 1854, in Peoria, Illinois, as part of the Lincoln-Douglas debates.

By March 4, 1861, when Lincoln stood on a platform on the east side of the Capitol to take the oath of office, the Union had already started to crumble. He pledged no interference with slavery "in the states where it exists," urging the nation to avert war and be touched "by the better angels of our nature."

A month later, Fort Sumter was fired on, and the country was enveloped in Civil War. On Capitol Hill arms merchants and would-be war speculators roamed the halls of Congress. The Navy Yard was open 24 hours a day, producing guns, shells, musket balls and percussion caps. The Marine Barracks housed troops and provided training, and many buildings on the Hill were commandeered by the military, including the bell tower of Christ Church on G Street, SE, which was used as an observation post.

Battles were fought nearby, and the wounded poured into the city. Providence Hospital, established in a renovated mansion at 2nd and D Streets, SE, had been in operation only six weeks when casualties from the first Battle of Bull Run were brought to Capitol Hill. Makeshift tent hospitals spread from the grounds of the Capitol to the square surrounding the new hospital, the city's only medical facility not taken over by the military during the Civil War. Providence Hospital was granted a congressional charter, signed by President Lincoln.

Military hospitals were built around the city and on Capitol Hill. One was located on the place on which Pierre L'Enfant had envisioned a monumental column from which all distances on the continent would be measured. No column was ever erected, and by the 1850s the area had become a dumping ground. The temporary medical facility built there was named Lincoln Hospital.

For a picture and more information on Lincoln Hospital, see page 92.

Congress also authorized a facility for treating wounded sailors and marines, but the Old Naval Hospital, the building that still stands at 9th and Pennsylvania, SE, was not ready for use until 18 months after Lee's surrender at Appomattox.

Since its beginnings, the city of Washington had been a major center for trading slaves, but that activity had ended as part of the Compromise of 1850, legislation that prevented the spread of slavery to the territories. Agitation to fully eradicate slavery here had been thwarted for decades by Southern members of Congress. But, with secession, those opponents were gone.

In the spring of 1862, Lincoln signed an act of Congress ending slavery in the District of Columbia. In the next few months, 930 slave owners who were loyal to the Union were compensated for the freedom of 2,989 slaves. Some of those freed joined First Regiment, U.S. Colored Troops, the black Civil War unit that was recruited and trained in Washington. The main recruiting station was Israel Bethel AME Church, located where the Rayburn House Office Building stands today.

Many children of the freed slaves were educated at Ebenezer Methodist Church in the 400 block of D Street, SE, which in 1864 set up the city's first publicly financed school for black children.

During the war, Lincoln was often at the Capitol to sign legislation and to borrow books from the congressional library. He frequently met with his friend John Dahlgren, commander of the Navy Yard, and watched the testing of ordinance. Lincoln and his advisors sometimes traveled by navy ship from the yard's port on the Anacostia to visit the troops, including a memorable trip during the Peninsula Campaign to confront General George McClellan about the progress of the war. This included one time when he viewed the testing of the Hyde Rocket, which exploded in its launcher. Fragments of the rocket narrowly missed the President.

On March 4, 1865, as the war neared its end, Lincoln once again was on Capitol Hill—delivering his famed Second Inaugural address, with the newly completed dome of the Capitol towering above the crowd. "With malice toward none; with charity for all; with firmness in the right, as God gives us to see the right, let us strive on to finish the work we are in."

A month later, Lincoln was killed by an assassin's bullet.

Our neighborhood's association with Lincoln continued. John Wilkes Booth's escape route carried him across Capitol Hill into Maryland. After he was killed, Booth's body was brought to the Navy Yard for an autopsy. The Old Arsenal, near the Hill in what is now Fort McNair, was the site for the trials and hanging of many conspirators in the assassination. And the Hill became the site of memorials to the martyred president.

In 1867, Congress renamed the area where Lincoln Hospital had stood Lincoln Square, the first site to bear his name. The Emancipation Statue, funded with contributions of freed slaves, was unveiled there on April 14, 1876, the 11th anniversary of Lincoln's death. Until the Lincoln Memorial was completed in 1922, this was the only place in Washington where visitors could pay homage to the martyred president.

April 16—the day that Lincoln signed legislation freeing the slaves in the District of Columbia—is now a holiday in the nation's capital.

The stain of slavery, embedded in the Constitution that was written in Philadelphia, was removed on Capitol Hill in Washington, D.C. It had been a long fight in the halls of Congress and the chambers of the Supreme Court, with many detours before the full promise of equality promised in the Declaration of Independence was fulfilled.

Neal Gregory, President
Friends of Southeast Library

January 20, 2009

"A View of the Capitol of the United States After the Conflagration in 1814." Frontispiece engraving from Jesse Torrey. *A Portraiture of Domestic Slavery in the United States*. Philadelphia: Jesse Torrey, publisher, 1817. (from New York Public Library via Google Books)

Torrey (1787–1834), a physician from Pennsylvania who traveled around the US to see slavery firsthand and write of its pernicious influence, was convinced that the burning of the Capitol during the War of 1812 was divine retribution for the United States's embracing of slavery.

Torrey spent some time in Washington, and described the scene depicted in the frontispiece thus: "On the 4th day of December, 1815, (the day on which the session of congress commenced,) being at the seat of government of the United States, I was preparing to enjoy the first opportunity that had occurred to me, of beholding the assembled representatives of the American republic. As I was about to proceed to the building where the session was opened, my agreeable reverie was suddenly interrupted by the voice of a stammering boy, who, as he was coming into the house, from the street exclaimed, 'There goes the Ge-Ge-orgy-men* with a drove o' niggers chain'd together two and two.' What's that, said I,—I must see,—and, going to the door, I just had a distant glimpse of a light covered waggon, followed by a procession of men, women and children, resembling that of a funeral. I followed them hastily; and as I approached so near as to discover that they were bound together in pairs, some with ropes, and some with iron chains, (which I had hitherto seen used only for restraining beasts,) the involuntary successive heavings of my bosom became irrepressible. This was, with me, an affection perfectly peculiar to itself, which never having before experienced, gave me some surprise. ... Overtaking the caravan, just opposite to the old capitol (then in a state of ruins from the conflagration by the British army,) I inquired of one of the drivers (of whom there were two) 'what part of the country they were taking all these people to?' 'To Georgia,' he replied. 'Have you not,' said I, 'enough such people in that country yet?' 'Not quite enough,' he said. I found myself incapable of saying more, and was compelled to avert my eyes immediately from the heart-rending scene!

"* On first hearing this epithet used, I was at a loss to account for its meaning. I have since observed that, in the middle states, the general title applied to slave-traders, indiscriminately, is 'Georgia-men.'"

Georgia was a frequent destination for slaves from Maryland and Virginia. These two states had been among the first to receive slaves, and had used their labor on large tobacco plantations. As tobacco became less lucrative, and—following the invention of the cotton gin—cotton began to grow in importance, there was a steady stream of slaves sold down South.

Table of Contents

"First Freed": Emancipation, April, 1862

Collective Memory, and Historical Realities in
Washington DC
John R. Wennersten

Emancipation came first to Washington in April, 1862, nine months before Lincoln's Emancipation Proclamation freed the slaves in the rebellious states of the Confederacy. In many respects emancipation in the District of Columbia was an experiment very much in the tradition of British racial emancipation in the Caribbean. It was a chance to see if financial compensation to slave owners in the District would ensure their loyalty to the Union. It was also an experiment insofar as the legal freeing of slaves in the District came with a strong caveat for the deportation of African-Americans abroad. Emancipation for the District in 1862 had little to do with either political morality or the future of Washington's freedmen.

While emancipation was welcomed in the African-American community and in the small community of northern abolitionists, most white people in the spring of 1862 were opposed to the implications and consequences of emancipation as well as the prospect of Black migration northward out of the District into the general great valley of central Pennsylvania. As freedmen drifted out of the District they would be more scorned as a workplace competitor than a new and helpful workforce.

Emancipation was not a new idea in 1862 either in the District or in the nation. Americans for decades had furiously debated the place of the African-American in American national life and the consequences of abolition in terms of political and civic equality in the United States. Economics lay at the heart of every emancipation scheme in the Western Hemisphere. As scholars have long noted, slaves were chattel, a form of property akin to real estate that was protected by the force of law. The freeing of slaves, accordingly, without full compensation was deemed illegal.

At the time of the legislation in 1862 freeing District bondsmen, the idea of emancipation was quite old, dating back to 1777

1

when Vermont proclaimed the abolition of slavery. Northern states like Pennsylvania, New York, and New Jersey followed suit. In these states, emancipation was a gradualist scheme that began with the emancipation of slave children and slaves. Slavery in this scheme was mandated to last only a generation more. By age 28, Pennsylvania slaves would become freedmen according to the 1780 statute. Slave owners not only in turn received a generation of slave labor in transition, they also received $3.50 a month for each slave child's care. As historian Claudia Goldin has noted, "this provision made the gradual abolition more palatable to the slave owners by enabling, in disguised form, some compensation."

Claudia Dale Goldin. "The Economics of Emancipation." *Journal of Economic History* 33.1, (1973): 69.

The story of emancipation in the British West Indies is better known. In 1834, Parliament bowed to the political pressure of British abolitionists and the realities of slave revolts in Jamaica and freed slaves under English dominion in the Caribbean. Slave owners received a compensation of twenty million pounds.

Even after the Civil War and the liberation of African-Americans in the United States, Cuba and Brazil retained their racial slave systems. In these two latter countries, a system of gradualist emancipation allowed planters in Cuba and Brazil to work their chattel for at least a generation. The introduction of government-sponsored Chinese labor in Cuba's sugar plantations and Italian labor in Brazil's coffee plantations softened the financial losses of emancipation.

Debating whether emancipation in the District of Columbia and beyond would have been possible without the Civil War is beyond the scope of this essay. Suffice it to say, the war did make many ideas feasible that in the 1850s were unthinkable. Emancipation in the District of Columbia differed from the general emancipation order signed by Lincoln. The District emancipation was a scheme based on the compensation of slave owners for their losses. The general Emancipation Proclamation that Lincoln signed after the battle of Antietam in 1862 did not provide compensation and Lincoln worried about the constitutionality of the document.

Slaves in the United States in 1860 on the eve of the Civil War constituted some $2.7 billion worth of capital and represented a daunting financial problem to all those who at the time advocated compensation schemes for eliminating slavery. As economists have noted, this $2.7 billion in capital cost had to be amortized with federal bonds at a time when the gross national product of the United States was only $4.2 billion. Further, practically every emancipation scheme contemplated by the 37th Congress in 1860 required gradual abolition followed by full emancipation over a

30 year period. Thus under this Congressional world-view all the slaves of the South would be freed by 1890. But it should be noted that this scheme, like most schemes under consideration by President Lincoln and the Congress, involved the colonization of the freedmen in Africa. Using the old figures of the American Colonization Society's "repatriation" costs of freedmen in Liberia in the 1820, this would have added an additional cost of $172 per person, a staggering sum. Finally, even if the money was available and all the ex-slaves wanted to be colonized in Africa, it is doubtful that the South would have been willing to relinquish a labor force of four million. One of the ironies of the Civil War is that it would have been far cheaper to pay for a scheme of emancipation than to wage a four year conflict that accomplished relatively little in politically and economically empowering the freedmen. Estimates by Professor Stanley Engerman and others put the cost of the Civil War at around $10 billion as opposed to compensated emancipation throughout the South at $2.7 billion. Few people with power and authority in the federal government actually sat down and realistically considered any plan of emancipation prior to 1862. Thus the emancipation of slaves in the District of Columbia in April, 1862 is a truly remarkable historical development and it is to the specifics of this eman-cipation of the "first freed" that we now turn.

The federally mandated emancipation document of April 16, 1862 entitled "An Act for the Release of certain persons held to Service or Labor in the District of Columbia" became law during a period of crisis in the District. Residents feared an immanent Confederate invasion and the Union Army, sluggish and ineptly led by General William B. McClellan was bogged down in the siege of Yorktown, Virginia. The town appeared overrun by "con-traband" or "escaped Negroes" and the financial community of the city was decidedly pro-Southern in its sympathies. Thus the emancipation of 1862 in the District was conditioned by realities that had relatively little to do with the moral predicament of African-American slaves in the federal city. Today a review of the legislation as contained in Executive Document No. 42 of the 38th Congress reveals, by our standards at least, an amazing mat-ter-of-factness in the face of an event of monumental proportions —the first legal freeing of slaves by the United States. Congress. Salmon P. Chase, Secretary of the Treasury at that time referred to the bill merely as a "report and tabular statements" for "the release of certain persons held to service or labor in the District of Columbia."

Section One of the legislation freed all slaves "by reason of African descent" in the District, except those who were convicted

Philip Staudenraus. *The African Colonization Movement, 1816–1865.* New York: Columbia University Press. 1961.

For more on the cost of Emancipation *vs.* the cost of the war, see letter on p. 144.

Emancipation in the District of Columbia, US House of Representa-tives, 38th Congress. 1st Session, Executive Document No. 42. See p. 73 for full text.

criminals. The legislation, in the following sections dealt with insuring the loyalties of slave owners in the District by setting up a special commission to take their oaths of loyalty to the United States government as a precondition to their receiving compensation for the loss of their bondsmen. No slave owner who has "borne arms against the government of the United States in the present rebellion" or who gave aid and comfort to the enemy was eligible for the program.

Once the above conditions were met, compensated emancipation in the District under this legislation was not to exceed $300 per slave. A three man Federal Emancipation Claims Commission appointed B.M. Campbell, an ex-slave trader from Baltimore, to authenticate and warrant emancipation financial claims to the federal government. The commission responded favorably to 909 compensation claims for 2,989 slaves from over 1,000 slave owners during the ninety days that followed the District Emancipation. The largest claim submitted was for 69 slaves from George Washington Young for the sum of $17,771.85. Most claims were for one or two slaves. Altogether slave owners in the District of Columbia received $993,406 in compensation for their slaves. Such a large award was without precedent in the history of racial slavery in the United States. Washington, DC was the only place in the United States where a full-fledged statutory compensated emancipation took place.

Ibid. The Youngs had been planters and slaveholders in the Anacostia region of Washington since the colonial period. Ownership of that number of slaves classified George Washington Young as a "slave magnate" and one of the South's wealthiest men. Only 6,000 families in the entire South owned 50 or more slaves.

Emancipation and Public Memory

Meanwhile, the collective public memory focuses on emancipation in the District of Columbia as somehow being a moral or "Godly" act. In the years since the Civil War ordinary people have conceived the past more to reflect the concerns of the present, specifically race relations and civil rights. Unfortunately, history, objectively conceived and sustained by the evidence, notes that there was little progress, either social or economic for the African-American in the United States from the period of the "first freedom" in the District of Columbia until the outbreak of World War I. Two world wars and the large northern migrations fostered African-Americans seeking new jobs and social opportunities. Ultimately, one can say that the African-American community was more liberated by the wars of the twentieth century than by the Civil War, despite the passage of the 14th and 15th Amendments to the Constitution which supposedly gave freedom and civil rights to the freedmen. Thus by looking at the emancipation of slaves in the District in 1862 as an act of commemoration, African-Americans can see in "first freedom" the origins of the values and aspirations they hold dear to today. The past in this manner becomes a process of engaging a difficult world and finding meaning in it.

The emancipation period takes on a different hue when we return to what Lincoln and others were actually saying in the lead-up to emancipation. While Lincoln was certainly willing to protect Black interests as a presidential war measure, this does not say much by today's standards. Lincoln always stressed that the Emancipation Proclamation was an act of military necessity and advocated deportation of the "captive people to their long-lost father land." (July 6, 1852, in his eulogy on Henry Clay)

Legislation for the District Emancipation allowed $100 in transportation allowance for freedmen wishing to emigrate to Africa. When Congress abolished slavery in the District of Columbia in April, 1862, Lincoln declared: "I am gratified that the two principles of compensation and colonization are both recognized in the act." Throughout Lincoln's public career he professed opposition to racial equality and never changed his views.

The Emancipation Memorial in Lincoln Park on Capitol Hill is a striking illustration of the collision of public memory and history over significant events and people. Designed and sculpted by Thomas Ball in 1876, the monument depicts President Abraham Lincoln holding the Emancipation Proclamation in his right hand. Beneath his hand is a plinth bearing patriotic symbols and a profile of George Washington, a Virginia slave owner. The "Great Emancipator" stands while freeing a crouching, shirtless and shackled slave. The statue sends many mixed cultural signals, and it has long been a source of controversy. At the statue's formal unveiling, Black abolitionist and orator Frederick A. Douglass said that "even here in the presence of the monument we have erected to his memory, Abraham Lincoln was not, in the fullest sense of the word, either our man or our model. In his interests, in his associations, in his habits of thought and in his prejudices, he was a white man. ... The race to which we belong were [sic] not the special objects of his consideration."

Many scholars since the post-Civil War period have criticized the statue for exemplifying a "suppliant and inferior posture of African-Americans." The statue is thus seen as a monument that perpetrates racist thought. A final source of culture clash surrounds the costs of the statue itself. Public memory records that the statue was built as a result of subscriptions raised from freed slaves, specifically from African-American veterans. While undoubtedly freedmen subscribed to the statue, the Western Sanitary Commission, a St. Louis-based volunteer war-relief agency run by white people, raised $20,000 for the statue. Thus the Emancipation Memorial was hardly a singular tribute to Abraham Lin-

"Eulogy on Henry Clay at Springfield, Illinois" *Speeches and Writings, 1832–1858.* Ed. Don E. Fehrenbacher. New York: Library of America,1989.

See p. 67 for the full text of Lincoln's message to Congress following the abolition of slavery in DC.

New York Times, April 22, 1876. For text of Douglass's speech, see p. 113.

coln by the freedmen of the United States.

While over the course of years new images of Lincoln have appeared in the context of African-American life, most of the times these images have fluctuated between the poles of racial assertiveness and accommodation, depending on the political tenor of the times and the conditions facing Black America. African-Americans have worked to embrace Abraham Lincoln by placing his memory in the context of their racial struggles.

The Abraham Lincoln Bicentennial

In the upcoming 2009 Bicentennial of Lincoln's birth, there will be elaborate ceremonies held at the Lincoln Memorial. One will be devoted to the spirit of democracy and national reconciliation that was the rationale for the memorial when it was dedicated in May, 1922. The other ceremony will highlight the concert that singer Marian Anderson gave on the steps of the Lincoln Memorial when racist factions in the Daughters of the American Revolution refused to provide her with a concert venue.

On Capitol Hill, African-American visitors to Lincoln Park will nod briefly at the Emancipation Memorial, reflect on slavery's brutal heritage and then proceed onward to the benign and optimistic statue of Mrs. Mary McLeod Bethune. This statue depicts an elderly Mrs. Bethune hands the legacy of "education" to two young Black children. The statue conveys a message of stewardship, tenderness and a devotion to a long career of education and civil rights.

Since 1974 the two "Emancipation Statues" have faced one another in the park, each one defined by both history and the public memory. Each statue carries its own distinct messages.

Resolution Offered by James Sloan

Annals of Congress, House of Representatives,
8ᵗʰ Congress, 2ⁿᵈ Session
January 18, 1805

The history of slavery is inextricably entwined with the history of the United States. Amongst the earliest immigrants were slaves, brought in 1619 to the Virginia colony. Though early slaves were, to some extent, indentured servants, both white and native American, the name soon stuck exclusively to people of African descent who had been brought against their will to America, and for whom there was no hope of liberty.

Although some territories and states banned slavery, there was no doubt that the new federal district would allow slavery within its borders. Both states which gave up land for it were slave-owning states, and, in fact, Virginia and Maryland's slave population made up half the total slaves in the United States in the year that Congress moved to the new Capital. Furthermore, the Constitution, in Article 4, Section 2, Clause 3, explicitly allowed slavery.

In spite of this, there was an abolitionist movement afoot in the United States even then. Either as a means to differentiate themselves from their British masters or in reaction to the noble words of the Declaration of Independence—or simply to answer Samuel Johnson's famous question "If slavery be thus fatally contagious, how is it that we hear the loudest yelps for liberty among the drivers of negroes?"—laws were passed by Congress infringing on some aspects of slavery.

In 1793, the US outlawed the slave trade, even tightening the law in 1800, banning all imports as of 1808. In spite of this and, possibly, because of this, the slave trade increased dramatically in these years, with as many slaves being brought into the country in the years 1780–1810 as had been imported in the preceding 160

The 1800 census showed there to be 887,612 slaves in the United States. Of these, 452,306 lived in Maryland and Virginia, with the vast majority in the latter state.

Dr. Samuel Johnson, *Taxation No Tyranny.* London, T. Cadell, 1775.

years. Furthermore, these laws, once actually in effect, did little to stop the importation of slaves—the last slave boat docked in 1859 in Mobile, Alabama—and did nothing to stop the institution of slavery.

At the same time, the Fugitive Slave Law of 1793, which cast into law the above clause of the constitution, showed clearly that, when it was a matter of siding with free or slave-holding states, it was the latter whose interests were chiefly respected.

It is therefore hardly surprising that James Sloan's bill, as reproduced below, was barely discussed and peremptorily voted down in 1805. Still, this bill represents the first attempt to free the slaves in the federal capital, setting into motion a process that would bear fruit 57 years later.

Sloan, who was considered by some to be the 'butt' of the Democratic-Republican party, remains a shadowy figure. No sources seem to agree on his birth and death date, but agree that he represented New Jersey in three Congresses, from 1803 to 1809.

Henry Adams, *History of the United States During the Second Administration of Thomas Jefferson.* New York: Scribner's, 1880, contains the pithy quote: "Sloan of New Jersey, a sort of butt in the party."

DISTRICT OF COLUMBIA

...

The fact that no number was indicated for the ages of males or females is normal in the writing of laws; very often, laws are introduced with such details left open and are filled in later by amendment.

Mr. Sloan moved the following resolution:

Resolved, That, from and after the fourth of July, 1805, all blacks and people of color, that shall be born within the District of Columbia, or whose mother shall be the property of any person residing within said District, shall be free, the males at the age of —, and the females at the age of —.

The House proceeded to consider the said motion, and on the question that the same be referred to to Committee of the whole House, it passed in the negative—yeas 47, nays 65, as follows:

[List of House members omitted]

And then the main question being taken that the House do agree to the said motion as originally proposed, it passed in the negative—yeas 31, nays 77, as follows:

[List of House members omitted]

So the said motion was rejected.

Memorial of Inhabitants of the District of Columbia Praying for the Gradual Abolition of Slavery in the District of Columbia

20th Congress, 1st Session, Doc. 215
March 24, 1828

The abolitionist movement in the District of Columbia began in earnest in 1827, with several societies engaged in that work being founded that year and the next year. The earliest DC-based group interested in these issues was the American Colonization Society whose members were intent on returning freed slaves to Africa. This group had been founded in 1816.

A common fixture of these early societies were 'Memorials,' which would today be called 'petitions,' consisting of a text describing the problem, as well as setting out the steps the undersigned were asking the group being lobbied to take.

An example of this was a memorial written and signed by 1,100 residents of the District of Columbia, requesting the abolition of slavery in their own city. Though the language is florid, and the appeal heartfelt, it should be noted that at least one of the undersigned continued to own slaves well after signing this document; he had a newspaper advertisement announcing a 300 dollar reward for the return of two of his slaves printed in 1842.

The list of these memorials, and the outrage presented within masks the true direction the federal government had taken in these years. In the words of Don Fehrenbacher, the government had become "to some degree a sponsor and protector of the institution [of slavery]" Fehrenbacher wrote these words in his study of the *Dred Scott* case, and expanded on the topic

Don E. Fehrenbacher. *The Dred Scott Case: Its significance in American Law and Politics.* NY: Oxford University Press, 1978.

Don E.
Fehrenbacher.
*The Slave-
holding Re-
public: An Ac-
count of the
United States
Government's
Relations to
Slavery.* NY,
Oxford Uni-
versity Press,
2001.

later: "[T]he antebellum United States ... was a slaveholding republic. That was the impression given by the national capital. That was the image presented in diplomacy to the rest of the world. And that had become the law of the land by edict of the Supreme Court."

It is in light of this attitude that the willingness of the citizens to sign their names to a document such as this should be regarded.

The petition itself was, like all others of the time, ignored by Congress.

MEMORIAL.

To the Honorable the Senate and House of Representatives of the United States of America in Congress assembled:

In 1828, the District of Columbia still included the portions of Virginia that had been turned over to the Federal government for the use by the federal city. This area, the County of Arlington, was returned to Virginia in 1834.
The true reasons for this retrocession remain hotly debated, but the fact that Alexandria was an important slave market is at least part of the reason.

We, the undersigned, citizens of the counties of Washington and Alexandria, in the District of Columbia, beg leave to call the attention of your honorable body to an evil of serious magnitude, which greatly impairs the prosperity and happiness of this District, and casts the reproach of inconsistency upon the free institutions established among us.

While the laws of the United States denounce the foreign slave trade as piracy, and punish with death those who are found engaged in its perpetration, there exists in this District, the Seat of the National Government, a domestic slave trade, scarcely less disgraceful in its character, and even more demoralizing in its influence. For this is not, like the former, carried on against a barbarous nation; its victims are reared up among the People of this country; educated in the precepts of the same religion; and imbued with similar domestic attachments.

These people are, without their consent, torn from their homes; husband and wife are frequently separated, and sold into distant parts; children are taken from their parents without regard to the ties of nature; and the most endearing bonds of affection are broken forever.

Nor is this traffic confined to those who are legally slaves for life. Some who are entitled to freedom, and many who have a limited time to serve, are sold into unconditional slavery, and, owing to the defectiveness of our laws, they are generally carried out of the District before the necessary steps can be taken for their release.

We behold these scenes continually taking place among us, and lament our inability to prevent them. The People of this District have, within themselves, no means of legislative redress, and we, therefore, appeal to your honorable body, as the only one invested by the American Constitution with the power to relieve us.

Nor is it only from the rapacity of slave traders that the colored race in this District are doomed to suffer. Even the laws which govern us, sanction and direct, in certain cases, a procedure that we believe is unparalleled in glaring injustice by any thing at present known among the Governments of Christendom. An instance of the operation of these laws, which occurred during the last Summer, we will briefly relate.

A colored man, who stated that he was entitled to freedom, was taken up as a runaway slave, and lodged in the jail of Washington City. He was advertised, but no one appearing to claim him, he was, according to law, put up at public auction, for the payment of his jail fees, and sold as a slave for life! He was purchased by a slave trader, who was not required to give security for his remaining in the District, and he was, soon after, shipped at Alexandria for one of the Southern States. An attempt was made by some benevolent individuals to have the sale postponed until his claim to freedom could be investigated, but their efforts were unavailing; and thus was a human being sold into perpetual bondage, at the capital of the freest Government on earth, without even a pretence of trial, or an allegation of crime.

We blush for our country while we relate this disgraceful transaction, and we would fain conceal it from the world, did not its very enormity inspire us with the hope that it will rouse the philanthropist and the patriot to exertion. We have no hesitation in believing your honorable body never intended that this odious law should be enforced; it was adopted with the old code of Maryland, from which, we believe, it has been expunged since this District was ceded to the General Government.

The fact of its having been so recently executed, shows the necessity of this subject being investigated by a power which we confidently hope will be ready to correct it.

We are aware of the difficulties that would attend any attempt to relieve us from these grievances by a sudden emancipation of the slaves in this District, and we would, therefore, be far from recommending so rash a measure. But the course pursued by many of the States of this Confederacy, that have happily succeeded in relieving themselves from a similar burden, together with the bright example which has been set us by the South American Republics, proves, most conclusively, that a course of gradual emancipation, to commence at some fixed period, and to take effect only upon those who may there. after be born or removed into the District, might be pursued, without detriment to

Which case, exactly, the writers of the memorial were referring to is not known. However, Rep. Charles Miner of Pennsylvania, in the course of an impassioned speech on the House floor on January 7, 1829, tells of at least five cases of free men being sold from the jails as slaves, and reads a letter describing the plight of one James Green, sold into slavery in the summer of 1827. The 'benevolent individuals' in that case were Ezekiel Young and Josiah Bosworth the present proprietors, and would greatly redound to the prosperity and honor of our country.

The existence among us of a distinct class of people, who, by their condition as slaves, are deprived of almost every incentive to virtue and industry, and shut out from many of the sources of light and knowledge, has an evident tendency to corrupt the morals of the people, and to damp the spirit of enterprise, by accustoming the rising generation to look with contempt upon honest labor, and to depend, for support, too much upon the labor of others. It prevents a useful and industrious class of people from settling among us, by rendering the means of subsistence more precarious to the laboring class of whites.

It diminishes the resources of the community, by throwing the earnings of the poor into the coffers of the rich; thus rendering the former dependent, servile, and improvident, while the latter are tempted to become, in the same proportion, luxurious and prodigal.

That these disastrous results flow from the existence of slavery among us, is sufficiently conspicuous, when we contrast the languishing condition of this District and the surrounding country, with the prosperity of those parts of the Union which are less favored in point of climate and location, but blessed with a free and industrious population.

We would, therefore, respectfully pray that these grievances may claim the attention of your honorable body, and that a law of Congress may be enacted, declaring that all children of slaves, born in the District of Columbia, after the fourth day of July, eighteen hundred and twenty-eight, shall be free at the age of twenty-five years; and that those laws which authorize the selling of supposed runaways for their prison fees or maintenance, may be repealed.

And, also, that laws may be enacted to prevent slaves from being removed into this District, or brought in for sale, hire, or transportation; without, however, preventing Members of Congress, resident strangers, or travellers, from bringing and taking away with them their domestic servants.

The vast majority of Africans taken from the homeland against their will and brought across the Atlantic ended up in the Caribbean and South America. Emancipation efforts in those regions began in 1804 (Haiti) and lasted until 1888 (Brazil)

Andrew Jackson was elected president the same year as this memorial was offered up; he ended up bringing slaves from home to work at the White House, housing them in the basement.

The Pinckney Resolutions

The Congressional Globe
May 25 & 26, 1836

The 1828 memorial marked the beginning of a deluge of petitions demanding emancipation into the House of Representatives (and, to a lesser extent, the Senate.) The historian Gilbert Barnes described the inundation of Congress by citizens protesting slavery thus: "outside the field of politics, it was the greatest project in propaganda that had ever been conceived in our history." During the first session of the 24th Congress (1835–36) about one hundred thousand signatures arrived asking for abolition in DC. Furthermore, abolitionist newspapers were ramping up their rhetoric denouncing the institution of slavery.

Gilbert Hobbs Barnes. *The Antislavery Impulse: 1830–1844.* Gloucester, Mass.: American Historical Association, 1933.

This pressure began to show on the floor of the House and Senate. On February 2, 1835, having introduced numerous petitions and memorials from citizens of New York, "one of which was signed by eight hundred ladies" seeking to ban slavery in the District of Columbia, Congressman John Dickson, Anti-Masonic member from New York, arose and gave an impassioned speech against the practice of jailing free Blacks and then selling them into slavery. The high point of his speech had him railing against the "man traps set at the seat of Government of this Republic, to seize and drag into perpetual bondage a freeman, entitled to all the rights and privileges of an American citizen."

John C. Rives. *Abridgment of the debates of Congress from 1789 to 1856, Vol. 12.* New York: D. Appleton, 1860.

That the Federal Government would ban slavery in the District of Columbia became a real fear of those whose livelihood depended on the continuation of slavery. As Mary Tremain describes it: "The determination to resist abolition in the District was not formed because they cared for [This should probably read 'about' –ed] slavery there. The three thousand slaves, more or less, made not the slightest difference

Mary Tremain
*Slavery in the
District of
Columbia:
The Policy of
Congress and
the Struggle
for Abolition.*
New York:
Putnam's,
1892.

to the Southern States. The claim that the District must be held as a necessary 'outpost' was absurd. They did not really believe that the government would interfere with slavery in the States: the most fanatical of the abolitionists never had claimed that the Constitution gave that right. The South depended even more than they professed to do upon moral support. They had persuaded themselves that slavery was right, or, at least, that it was a less evil than emancipation. Slavery in the District served merely as a gauge by which to measure the anti-slavery sentiment of the country. As soon as a majority of the nation should be induced to declare not merely the abstract principle that slavery was wrong, but that it could and should be remedied by legislation, the position of the South would be shaken. Because of the moral influence in their own States of such a declaration, they were determined it should not be made. This is precisely the reason, also, that the abolitionists were so persistent."

As the debate over slavery became ever more likely to end with at least a limited ban on slavery, the pro-slavery forces did what they could to squelch all debate on the subject. One of their tactics was to pass a resolution that denied any "petitions, memorials, resolutions, propositions, or papers" that had anything to do with slavery from being acted upon; they were to be tabled without discussion.

For informa-
tion about
Pinckney's fa-
ther and his at-
titude towards
slaves, see p.
89.

One set of such resolutions was introduced in 1836 by South Carolina Representative Henry Laurens Pinckney. The first resolution was voted on on May 25, and passed by an overwhelming 182-9 vote, though a number of Congressmen refused to vote. One of the few on the losing side, and vocal critic of all three resolutions, was ex-President John Quincy Adams. The second two resolutions passed the next day, by somewhat closer 132-45 and 117-68 margins. The last was known from then on as the "Gag Rule."

The first at-
tempt to intro-
duce the 21st
Rule precipi-
tated an imme-
diate filibuster
by William
Slade, Repre-
sentative from
Vermont.
*Congressional
Globe*, 26th
Congress, 1st
Session.

Since these were resolutions, they were good only for the session of Congress that passed them, and had to be re-passed each year. The speed with which these resolutions passed increased by the years, limiting the debate on the debate, as well. By 1840, the pro-Slavery Representatives managed to pass a house rule, which did not have to be re-introduced every year. The margin by which this rule—generally referred to as the 21st rule —was enacted was considerably less than that which the Pinckney gag resolution had passed.

The gag rule was eventually rescinded in 1844.

The resolutions presented here are taken from *The Congressional Globe*, which, from 1833–1873 printed all the discussions in Congress, as is now done by the *Congressional Record*. The text is from page 498 of the *Globe* for the 24th Congress, 1st Session.

Resolved, That Congress possesses no constitutional authority to interfere in any way with the institution of slavery in any if the states of this Confederacy.

Resolved, That Congress ought not to interfere in any way with slavery in the District of Columbia.

And whereas it is extremely important and desirable that the agitation of this subject should be finally arrested, for the purpose of restoring tranquillity to the public mind, your committee respectfully recommend the adoption of the following additional resolution, viz:

Resolved, That all petitions, memorials, resolutions, propositions, or papers, relating in any way, or to any extent whatever, to the subject of slavery, or the abolition of slavery, shall, without being either printed or referred, be laid upon the table, and that no further action whatever shall be had thereon.

Having a bill or petition etc. 'laid on the table' meant that no further action would be taken on it.

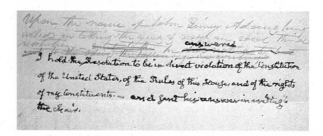

John Quincy Adams's reply to the gag rule. When called upon to vote, he instead issued this statement: "I hold the resolution to be in direct violation of the Constitution of the United States, of the rules of this House, and of the rights of my Constituents and I give this answer in writing to the chair." (from National Archives)

Duff Green's Row in the late 19th Century. The boarding house that Lincoln and his family lived in while on Capitol Hill is the second from the left (Twitchell's Capital Business College, to the left of the 'Architect' in this picture.) The road visible behind the houses is A Street SE. This section of road no longer exists, as the entire site is covered by the original Library of Congress building. See also map in the frontispiece. (from Library of Congress)

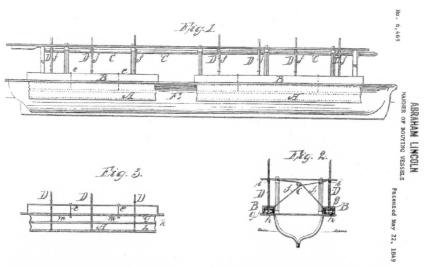

Abraham Lincoln's patent. Front page of patent application filed by Abraham Lincoln March 10, 1849. The patent described a new way of lifting boats over shoals through the use of "adjustable buoyant air chambers," and was inspired by having Lincoln's boat run aground during his trip home between congressional sessions. The patent was approved May 22, 1849, but was never marketed. Nonetheless, Lincoln remains the only President ever to have received a patent. (from Google Patents)

Abraham Lincoln on Capitol Hill

Robert Pohl

On November 25, 1847, Lincoln, his wife and two children left Lexington, Kentucky for Washington DC, where Lincoln was to begin his term as Congressman from the 7th Congressional district of Illinois. The trip took about a week, probably first by stagecoach to Winchester, Virginia, thereafter by train.

The Lincoln family arrived in Washington DC on December 2, 1847, where they registered at Brown's Hotel in the 600 block of Pennsylvania Ave NW. The hotel was already famous at the time as the place that John Tyler was administered the oath of office in 1841 after the death of William Henry Harrison, as well as having been the site of the inaugural ball for President James Monroe in 1821.

Lincoln and his family stayed only for one night before moving to Mrs. Sprigg's boardinghouse. Mrs. Sprigg, the widow of Major Benjamin Sprigg, had been taking lodgers since the death of her husband in 1833.

The boardinghouse was part of "Duff Green's Row," five houses stretching along the east side of 1st St between East Capitol and A Streets SE. The row of houses was originally known as "Carroll Row," as they had been built with the investment of Daniel Carroll of Duddington, who was a large landowner in the area. The row was later bought by Duff Green, the editor of the *United States Telegraph* newspaper, giving it its new name. Green lived in the southern-most house, but took his meals at Mrs. Sprigg's, which was the second from the north of the row.

Lincoln lived with numerous other Congressional Whigs in a "mess," as this arrangement was called. He shared his house with Reps. John Blanchard, John Dickey, Abraham McIlvaine, John Strohm, and James Pollock of Pennsylvania, as well as Joshua Giddings (Ohio), Elisha Embree (Indiana), and Patrick Tompkins (Mississippi), and was known as a superb raconteur who kept his fellow lodgers in good spirits through the long nights.

It was not just over the dinner table that Lincoln's ability as a storyteller was known, as this story, written by Benjamin Poore, a newspaper correspondent, shows:

Benjamin Perley Poore, "Lincoln and the Newspaper Correspondents." *Reminiscences of Abraham Lincoln by Distinguished Men of His Time.* Ed. Allen Thorndike Rice. New York: Harper & Brothers, 1909.

During the Christmas holidays Mr. Lincoln found his way into the small room used as the post-office of the House, where a few jovial *raconteurs* used to meet almost every morning, after the mail had been distributed into the members' boxes, to exchange such new stories as any of them might have acquired since they had last met. After modestly standing at the door for several days, Mr. Lincoln was "reminded" of a story, and by New Year's he was recognized as the champion story-teller of the Capitol. His favorite seat was at the left of the open fire-place, tilted back in his chair, with his long legs reaching over to the chimney jamb. He never told a story twice, but appeared to have an endless repertoire of them, always ready, like the successive charges in a magazine gun, and always pertinently adapted to some passing event.

Just as he had patiently waited for an opening to speak in the mail room, so did Lincoln carefully plan his speeches on the House floor. On December 27, 1847, Lincoln requested permission to speak for the first time, to present a petition.

Later that day, Lincoln gave notice of his intention to file a bill that would amend the act which had allowed for the raising of extra soldiers to fight the Mexican-American War. The war and its aftermath were frequently debated in Congress, and slavery had become an issue with the famous Wilmot proviso, which would have barred slavery from the newly-gained territories.

Lincoln is variously (most famously by Douglas during their debates) quoted as saying that he had voted for the Wilmot proviso "about forty-two times" in the course of his Congressional term.

On January 12, 1848, he followed through on his intention. The bill was read twice and committed to the the Committee of the Whole House on the state of the Union. The bill ensured that soldiers holding bounty land or scrip would not lose this due to their promotion to the rank of an officer, instead, this should be taken as an honorable discharge. There is no indication that it was ever debated or voted on.

Finally, on January 5, 1848, Lincoln gave his first proper speech. During the debates on "The Great Southern Mail," Lincoln arose and discussed the fare rates as proposed by the Postmaster General. The speech was not a memorable one, either for the contents or, apparently, for its delivery. Lincoln critiqued himself three days later in a letter to William Herndon, his law partner in Springfield:

As to speech-making, by way of getting the hang of the House, I made a little speech two or three days ago on a post-office question of no general interest. I find speaking here and elsewhere about the same thing. I was about as badly scared, and no worse, as I am when I speak in court. I expect to make one within a week or two in which I hope to succeed well enough to wish you to see it.

The speech which Lincoln planned to make "within a week or two" is one he gave on January 12, and it was indeed a barn-burner. In it, he took President Polk to task about the start of the Mexican-American war, demanding that President Polk describe exactly where the Americans killed by the Mexicans, the *casus belli*, were when they died. The reaction to this speech was described by Dr. Samuel Busey, a fellow boarder at Mrs Sprigg's.

I recall with vivid pleasure the scene of merriment at the dinner after his first speech in the House of Representatives, occasioned by the descriptions, by himself and others of the Congressional mess, of the uproar in the House during its delivery.

Dr. Busey also charmingly describes Lincoln's penchant for bowling at an alley right around the corner from his home, on A Street, between 1st Street and New Jersey Avenue:

Congressman Lincoln was very fond of bowling, and would frequently join others of the mess, or meet other members in a match game, at the alley of James Casparis, which was near the boarding-house. He was a very awkward bowler, but played the game with great zest and spirit, solely for exercise and amusement, and greatly to the enjoyment and entertainment of the other players and bystanders by his criticisms and funny illustrations. He accepted success and defeat with like good nature and humor, and left the alley at the conclusion of the game without a sorrow or disappointment. When it was known that he was in the alley there would assemble numbers of people to witness the fun which was anticipated by those who knew of his fund of anecdotes and jokes. When in the alley, surrounded by a crowd of eager listeners, he indulged with great freedom in the sport of narrative, some of which were very broad. His witticisms seemed for the most part to be impromptu, but he always told the anecdotes and jokes as if he wished to convey the impression that he had heard them from some one; but they appeared very many times as if they had been made for the immediate occasion.

"January 8, 1848—Letter to William H. Herndon." *Abraham Lincoln: Complete Works, Comprising His Speeches, Letters, State Papers, and Miscellaneous Writings, Volume 1.* Ed. John G. Nicolay, and John Hay. New York: The Century Co., 1907.

Dr. Samuel C Busey. *Personal Reminiscences and Recollections of Forty-Six Years' Membership in the Medical Society of the District of Columbia and Residence in This City,* Philadelphia: Dornan, Printer, 1895.

There are plenty of indications that Lincoln partook in the social whirl that was Washington. He attended a performances of the "Ethiopian Serenaders," a blackface minstrel troupe as well as concerts on the Capitol grounds. Furthermore, Lincoln was made one of the managers of the "Birth Night Ball," in which money was raised for the Washington Monument, which was to be held on February 22.

On February 21, while Lincoln was on the House floor, former President and now Representative John Quincy Adams suffered a stroke from which he did not recover. Lincoln was named to the committee tasked with the arrangements of Adams's funeral, though by his own admission, Lincoln's involvement were negligible:

"To Rev. Henry Slicer." *Uncollected Letters of Abraham Lincoln.* Ed. Gilbert Avery Tracy. New York: Houghton Mifflin Company, 1917.

As I remember, the House ordered the raising of two committees, one of Arrangements, number indefinite, the other, thirty in number, to attend the remains of Mr. Adams to Massachusetts. By some mistake, as I understood, a committee of thirty was appointed by the Speaker, as a committee of Arrangements, of which I was a member. At our first meeting, the mistake was discovered, and the committee being much too numerous for convenience, we delegated our authority to a subcommittee, of a smaller number of our own body, of which sub-committee, I was not a member. Whatever was done in the matter about which you enquire, I presume was done by the sub-committee; at all events, I have no knowledge of it whatever.

On Saturday the 26th, then, after funeral services in the House of Representatives, a large procession—including Lincoln—accompanied the body of the former President down East Capitol Street and so to Congressional Cemetery, at 18th and E Streets SE, where he was placed in the public vault.

Because of Adams's death and funeral, the Birth Night Ball was postponed to March 1.

Most of what Lincoln did in his first term had to do with discussions of the Mexican-American war and its aftermath, due to his membership in the Committee on Expenditures in the War Department. Otherwise, he was busy with Postal issues stemming from his spot on the Post Office and Post Road committee, constituent work, and, of course, the question of slavery.

The latter issue had come up almost immediately. On December 21, Lincoln voted against tabling a petition from DC inhabitants requesting the end of the slave trade in their city. Nine days later, he again voted against the tabling of a request to use monies received from land sales to help in the "extinction of slavery in

Congressional Globe, 30th Congress, 1st Session.

the US." In both cases, Lincoln voted with the minority, and neither petition was considered any further.

Less than a month later, the issue of slavery in general, and its influence in the District of Columbia in general, was brought home during an incident at Mrs. Sprigg's boardinghouse, which Joshua Giddings described on the floor of the House three days later:

> [O]n Friday last three armed persons, engaged in the internal slave trade, entered a dwelling in this city, and violently seized a colored man, employed as a waiter in the boarding-house of several members of this body, and, in the presence of his wife, gagged him, placed him in irons, and with loaded pistols, forced him into one of the slave prisons of this city, from which, it is reported, he has since been despatched for the slave market at New Orleans;
>
> [S]aid colored man had been employed in said boarding-house for several years, had become well and favorably known to members of this House, had married wife in this city and, under a contract to purchase his freedom for the sum of $300, had, by great industry, paid that sum within $60;

Congressional Globe, 30th Congress, 1st Session.

Although the resolution Giddings offered—which would have either appointed a select committee to look into repealing the laws in DC upholding slavery, or "removed the seat of Government to some free State"—was not passed, Lincoln, who may or may not have been present during the incident but certainly would have known the waiter, voted in all cases with his mess-mate.

In fact Lincoln, who was personally deeply against slavery and particularly opposed to its spreading into new territory, generally voted for the abolitionist side. When he did not support the abolitionist side, there was usually a judicious reason for him not to do so. Two instances stand out in this regard.

Lincoln voted to table debate in one case where Rep. John G. Palfrey from Massachusetts moved to add a resolution to the previous day's resolution congratulating the people of France on their new, republican, government. Palfrey asked that the words "Resolved, That no despotism is more effective than that which exists under the semblance of popular institutions" be added. This engendered a long discussion on, of course, slavery, and, in the end, the motion was voted down with the help of a vote from Representative Lincoln.

Ibid.

See page 41 for more on the *Pearl* incident and its aftermath.

Two weeks thereafter, a discussion about the *Pearl* incident was tabled, once again with Lincoln's concurring vote, after Representative Albert G. Brown from Mississippi requested that the subject be dropped so as to keep it from going "to the country to a greater extent than it had already gone out."

Lincoln showed himself a hard-working Representative in other ways, too. The only time he missed any House business during the first session is when he went to the the the Whig convention in Philadelphia for a few days in June 1848. He also missed a few days at the beginning of the second session when returning from Illinois.

The second, shorter, session gave Lincoln more opportunities to vote on the slavery issue, and also has the distinction of being the session in which Lincoln first introduced a bill having to do with it. He started the session by twice voting against bills that would have affected slavery in the District of Columbia: On December 18. 1848, he voted to table Rep. Giddings's bill to allow for a referendum on slavery in the District, and three days later, he voted against a resolution asking the Committee on the District of Columbia to compose a bill banning slavery there.

However, in both cases he may have been voting against them not because he felt there was no need to abolish slavery in the District, but rather that they went about it the wrong way, for on January 10, 1849, the following exchange took place on the House floor:

Congressional Globe, 30th Congress, 2nd Session Jan 10, 1849. All brackets in original.

John Wentworth (1815–1888) was the Representative from Illinois's 4th District in 1849. He was later Mayor of Chicago before returning to the House in 1865.

Mr. Lincoln appealed to his colleague [Mr. Wentworth] to withdraw his motion, to enable him to read a proposition which he intended to submit, if the vote should be reconsidered.

Mr. Wentworth again withdrew his motion for that purpose.

Mr. Lincoln said, that by the courtesy of his colleague, he would say, that if the vote on the resolution was reconsidered, he should make an effort to introduce an amendment, which he should now read.

And Mr. L. read as follows:

Strike out all after the word "Resolved" and insert the following:

"That the Committee on the District of Columbia be instructed to report a bill in substance as follows:

"Section 1 *Be it enacted by the Senate and House of Representatives of the United States of America in Congress assembled*: That no person not now within the District of Columbia, nor now owned by any person or persons now resident within it, nor hereafter born within it, shall ever be held in slavery within said District.

"Sec. 2. That no person now within said District, or

now owned by any person, or persons now resident within the same, or hereafter born within it, shall ever be held in slavery without the limits of said District: *Provided*, that officers of the Government of the United States, being citizens of the slave-holding states, coming into said District on public business, and remaining only so long as may be reasonably necessary for that object, may be attended into, and out of, said District, and while there, by the necessary servants of themselves and their families, without their right to hold such servants in service, being thereby impaired.

"Sec. 3 That all children born of slave mothers within said District on, or after the first day of January in the year of our Lord one thousand, eight hundred and fifty shall be free; but shall be reasonably supported and educated, by the respective owners of their mothers or by their heirs or representatives, and shall owe reasonable service, as apprentices, to such owners, heirs and representatives until they respectively arrive at the age of — years when they shall be entirely free; and the municipal authorities of Washington and Georgetown, within their respective jurisdictional limits, are hereby empowered and required to make all suitable and necessary provisions for enforcing obedience to this section, on the part of both masters and apprentices.

"Sec. 4. That all persons now within said District lawfully held as slaves, or now owned by any person or persons now resident within said District, shall remain such, at the will of their respective owners, their heirs and legal representatives: *Provided* that any such owner, or his legal representative, may at any time receive from the treasury of the United States the full value of his or her slave, of the class in this section mentioned, upon which such slave shall be forthwith and forever free: *and provided further* That the President of the United States, the Secretary of State, and the Secretary of the Treasury shall be a board for determining the value of such slaves as their owners may desire to emancipate under this section; and whose duty it shall be to hold a session for the purpose, on the first Monday of each calendar month; to receive all applications; and, on satisfactory evidence in each case, that the person presented for valuation, is a slave, and of the class in this section mentioned, and is owned by the applicant, shall value such slave at his or her full cash value, and give to the applicant an order on the treasury for the amount; and

None of the states who had emancipated their slaves had attempted to compensate their owners. Compensated Emancipation Bills were introduced in Maryland and Missouri in 1861, but failed to pass.

Section 6 requires that a majority of 'free white male citizens' over 21 must agree to this bill in order for it to take effect. It was by no means a given that the voters would have voted to abolish slavery. While most seemed to feel that the current treatment of freedmen was overly harsh, the attitude towards slavery itself was not as negative. Though over a thousand had signed a petition in 1828, later petitions drew fewer signatures, and it was often said that "the inhabitants [of the District] had not asked for abolition, and did not want it." (Tremain. *Slavery in the District of Columbia.* New York: Putnam's, 1892.) See also p. 55.

also to such slave a certificate of freedom.

"Sec. 5 That the municipal authorities of Washington and Georgetown, within their respective jurisdictional limits, are hereby empowered and required to provide active and efficient means to arrest, and deliver up to their owners, all fugitive slaves escaping into said District.

"Sec. 6 That the election officers within said District of Columbia, are hereby empowered and required to open polls at all the usual places of holding elections, on the first Monday of April next, and receive the vote of every free white male citizen above the age of twenty-one years, having resided within said District for the period of one year or more next preceding the time of such voting, for, or against this act; to proceed, in taking said votes, in all respects not herein specified, as at elections under the municipal laws; and, with as little delay as possible, to transmit correct statements of the votes so cast to the President of the United States. And it shall be the duty of the President to canvass said votes immediately, and, if a majority of them be found to be for this act, to forthwith issue his proclamation giving notice of the fact; and this act shall only be in full force and effect on, and after the day of such proclamation.

"Sec. 7. That involuntary servitude for the punishment of crime, whereof the party shall have been duly convicted shall in no wise be prohibited by this act.

"Sec. 8. That for all the purposes of this act the jurisdictional limits of Washington are extended to all parts of the District of Columbia not now included within the present limits of Georgetown."

Mr. LINCOLN then said, that he was authorized to say, that of about fifteen of the leading citizens of the District of Columbia to whom this proposition had been submitted, there was not one but who approved of the adoption of such a proposition. He did not wish to be misunderstood. He did not know whether or not they would vote for this bill on the first Monday of April; but he repeated, that out of fifteen persons to whom it had been submitted, he had authority to say that every one of them desired that some proposition like this should pass.

[Several voices: "Who are they? Give us their names."]

Lincoln had written this bill long before the resolution that he attempted to replace with it was introduced, which is why he had a fully-fledged document to share. He had, as he stated, spoken with a number of DC residents, not the least of which was the current Mayor, Colonel William Seaton, as well as his mess-mate at Mrs. Sprigg's, Rep. Giddings, known as the lead abolitionist in the House.

Giddings, in his diary, describes the situation after Lincoln's attempt to introduce his bill:

> "This evening (January 11), our whole mess remained in the dining-room after tea, and conversed upon the subject of Mr. Lincoln's bill to abolish slavery. It was approved by all; I believe it as good a bill as we could get at this time, and am willing to pay for slaves in order to save them from the Southern market, as I suppose every man in the District would sell his slaves if he saw that slavery was to be abolished."

John G. Nicolay and John Hay. *Abraham Lincoln: A History – Volume 1.* New York: The Century Company, 1890. The excerpt from Giddings's diary is on pages 195–196.

Buoyed by these varied sources of approval, Lincoln then, on January 13, gave notice that he would be introducing this compensated emancipation bill. Though there is no indication in the *Globe* that anything further happened with this bill, Nicolay and Hay write what really happened.

> But the usual result followed as soon as it was formally introduced to the notice of Congress. It was met by that violent and excited opposition which greeted any measure, however intrinsically moderate and reasonable, which was founded on the assumption that slavery was not in itself a good and desirable thing. The social influences of Washington were brought to bear against a proposition which the Southerners contended would vulgarize society, and the genial and liberal mayor was forced to withdraw his approval as gracefully or as awkwardly as he might. The prospects of the bill were seen to be hopeless, as the session was to end on the 4th of March, and no further effort was made to carry it through.

Ibid. p287ff.

John G. Nicolay and John Hay were Lincoln's secretaries.

With the session ended, Lincoln's first act as a private citizen was to attend the inauguration of Zachary Taylor, an event described by his colleague Representative Washburne of Illinois as follows:

> I was again in Washington part of the winter of 1849 (after the election of General Taylor), and saw much of Mr. Lincoln. A small number of mutual friends—including Mr. Lincoln—made up a party to attend the inauguration ball together. It was by far the most brilliant inauguration ball ever given. Of course Mr. Lincoln had never seen anything of the kind before. One of the most modest and un-

Elihu Benjamin Washburne. "Political Life in Illinois." *Reminiscences of Abraham Lincoln by*

Distinguished Men of His Time. Ed. Allen Thorndike Rice. New York: Harper & Brothers, Publishers, 1909.

pretending persons present—he could not have dreamed that like honors were to come to him, almost within a little more than a decade. He was greatly interested in all that was to be seen, and we did not take our departure until three or four o'clock in the morning. When we went to the cloak and hat room, Mr. Lincoln had no trouble in finding his short cloak, which little more than covered his shoulders, but, after a long search, was unable to find his hat. After an hour he gave up all idea of finding it. Taking his cloak on his arm, he walked out into Judiciary Square, deliberately adjusting it on his shoulders, and started off bareheaded for his lodgings. It would be hard to forget the sight of that tall and slim man, with his short cloak thrown over his shoulders, starting for his long walk home on Capitol Hill, at four o'clock in the morning, without any hat on.

His term as a Congressman over, there was nothing for Lincoln to do but to return to being a lawyer. His first case—argued four days after Lincoln's Congressional term was up—kept him right on Capitol Hill, however, as he argued a case before the Supreme Court. Lincoln worked for the defendant, Thomas Lewis, in the case of *William Lewis, for use of Nicholas Longworth vs. Thomas Lewis, administrator of Broadwell*. The case revolved around a breach of contract as well as the statute of limitations, and at what point a newer law superseded an older one.

The case is also known as *Lewis v. Lewis* as well as *Lewis, for the Use of of Longworth v. Lewis*; the Supreme Court citation is *Lewis v. Lewis* 48 US 776 (1849). Lincoln eventually worked on six Supreme Court cases. This was the only one he argued in person.

While waiting for the justices to decide the case, Lincoln applied for the patent shown at the beginning of this chapter. Three days later, the Supreme Court ruled against him, though dissenting judge, Justice McLean, wrote a long dissent which was based on Lincoln's argument.

With this piece of business finished, Lincoln returned to Springfield.

Within a few months, though, Lincoln was back in Washington DC, this time in a ultimately futile attempt to secure for himself the job of Commissioner of the Grant Land Office. Shortly after his arrival, in mid-June of 1849, Chicago attorney Justin Butterfield was given the job, and Lincoln returned again to Springfield. He would not return to Washington until February 23, 1861, 10 days before his inauguration as 16th President of the United States.

The Kidnapping and Sale of Solomon Northup

Twelve Years a Slave
1855

A few years after the publication of Harriet Beecher Stowe's anti-slavery novel *Uncle Tom's Cabin* in 1852, another story which similarly galvanized public opinion was splashed through the newspapers. In 1841, a free man named Solomon Northup (though the *New York Times* consistently calls him Northrup) from upstate New York had been brought to Washington DC under false pretenses, kidnapped, and sold into slavery. He was rescued 12 years later after a letter from him reached his wife and he was brought back to DC to charge his kidnappers.

In contrast to the *Pearl* incident described in the next chapter, the public knew nothing of Northup's predicament until after his release. Newspaper stories began to appear in January, 1853, and by 1854, a *New York Times* article describing sentiments in England mentioned *Uncle Tom's Cabin* and Northup in a single sentence. That his plight made in impression on the reading public is clear, in 1857, another *Times* article mentions him as being 'fresh in the reader's mind.'

In this excerpt from his memoirs, Northup describes what happened to him in Washington DC, where he was kept and how he was treated. Included are parts of Chapters 2 and 4, as well as the whole of Chapter 3.

Brown and Hamilton are Merrill Brown and Abram Hamilton, though there is no indication that these are their real names.

Solomon Northup. *Twelve Years a Slave: Narrative of Solomon Northup, a Citizen of New-York, Kidnapped in Washington City in 1841 and Rescued in 1853, from a Cotton Plantation Near the Red River, in Louisiana.* New York: Miller, Orton & Mulligan, 1855.

We [Northup, Brown and Hamilton] left the carriage at Baltimore, and entering the cars, proceeded to Washington, at which

27

place we arrived just at nightfall, the evening previous to the funeral of General Harrison, and stopped at Gadsby's Hotel, on Pennsylvania Avenue.

After supper they called me to their apartments, and paid me forty-three dollars, a sum greater than my wages amounted to, which act of generosity was in consequence, they said, of their not having exhibited as often as they had given me to anticipate, during our trip from Saratoga. They moreover informed me that it had been the intention of the circus company to leave Washington the next morning, but that on account of the funeral, they had concluded to remain another day. They were then, as they had been from the time of our first meeting, extremely kind. No opportunity was omitted of addressing me in the language of approbation; while, on the other hand, I was certainly much prepossessed in their favor. I gave them my confidence without reserve, and would freely have trusted them to almost any extent. Their constant conversation and manner towards me—their foresight in suggesting the idea of free papers, and a hundred other little acts, unnecessary to be repeated—all indicated that they were friends indeed, sincerely solicitous for my welfare. I know not but they were. I know not but they were innocent of the great wickedness of which I now believe them guilty. Whether they were accessory to my misfortunes—subtle and inhuman monsters in the shape of men—designedly luring me away from home and family, and liberty, for the sake of gold—those these read these pages will have the same means of determining as myself. If they were innocent, my sudden disappearance must have been unaccountable indeed; but revolving in my mind all the attending circumstances, I never yet could indulge, towards them, so charitable a supposition.

After receiving the money from them, of which they appeared to have an abundance, they advised me not to go into the streets that night, inasmuch as I was unacquainted with the customs of the city. Promising to remember their advice, I left them together, and soon after was shown by a colored servant to a sleeping room in the back part of the hotel, on the ground floor. I laid down to rest, thinking of home and wife, and children, and the long distance that stretched between us, until I fell asleep. But no good angel of pity came to my bedside, bidding me to fly—no voice of mercy forewarned me in my dreams of the trials that were just at hand.

The next day there was a great pageant in Washington. The roar of cannon and the tolling of bells filled the air, while many houses were shrouded with crape, and the streets were black with people. As the day advanced, the procession made its appearance, coming slowly through the Avenue, carriage after carriage, in

There were actually two Gadsby Hotels on Pennsylvania Avenue: One at 3rd Street, the other at 6th. The former was run by the son of the proprietor of the latter.

William Henry Harrison, who had been a general in the war of 1812, died on April

long succession, while thousands upon thousands followed on foot—all moving to the sound of melancholy music. They were bearing the dead body of Harrison to the grave.

From early in the morning, I was constantly in the company of Hamilton and Brown. They were the only persons I knew in Washington. We stood together as the funeral pomp passed by. I remember distinctly how the window glass would break and rattle to the ground, after each report of the cannon they were firing in the burial ground. We went to the Capitol, and walked a long time about the grounds. In the afternoon, they strolled towards the President's House, all the time keeping me near to them, and pointing out various places of interest. As yet, I had seen nothing of the circus. In fact, I had thought of it but little, if at all, amidst the excitement of the day.

My friends, several times during the afternoon, entered drinking saloons, and called for liquor. They were by no means in the habit, however, so far as I knew them, of indulging to excess. On these occasions, after serving themselves, they would pour out a glass and hand it to me. I did not become intoxicated, as may be inferred from what subsequently occurred. Towards evening, and soon after partaking of one of these potations, I began to experience most unpleasant sensations. I felt extremely ill. My head commenced aching—a dull, heavy pain, inexpressibly disagreeable. At the supper table, I was without appetite; the sight and flavor of food was nauseous. About dark the same servant conducted me to the room I had occupied the previous night. Brown and Hamilton advised me to retire, commiserating me kindly, and expressing hopes that I would be better in the morning. Divesting myself of coat and boots merely, I threw myself upon the bed. It was impossible to sleep. The pain in my head continued to increase, until it became almost unbearable. In a short time I became thirsty. My lips were parched. I could think of nothing but water—of lakes and flowing rivers, of brooks where I had stooped to drink, and of the dripping bucket, rising with its cool and overflowing nectar, from the bottom of the well. Towards midnight, as near as I could judge, I arose, unable longer to bear such intensity of thirst. I was a stranger in the house, and knew nothing of its apartments. There was no one up, as I could observe. Groping about at random, I knew not where, I found the way at last to a kitchen in the basement. Two or three colored servants were moving through it, one of whom, a woman, gave me two glasses of water. It afforded momentary relief, but by the time I had reached my room again, the same burning desire of drink, the same tormenting thirst, had again returned. It was even more torturing than before, as was also the wild pain in my head,

4, 1841, after serving all of 30 days as President. He was buried in Ohio after the procession on April 7 through DC.

if such a thing could be. I was in sore distress—in most excruciating agony! I seemed to stand on the brink of madness! The memory of that night of horrible suffering will follow me to the grave.

In the course of an hour or more after my return from the kitchen, I was conscious of some one entering my room. There seemed to be several—a mingling of various voices,—but how many, or who they were, I cannot tell. Whether Brown and Hamilton were among them, is a mere matter of conjecture. I only remember with any degree of distinctness, that I was told it was necessary to go to a physician and procure medicine, and that pulling on my boots, without coat or hat, I followed them through a long passage-way, or alley, into the open street. It ran out at right angles from Pennsylvania Avenue. On the opposite side there was a light burning in a window. My impression is there were then three persons with me, but it is altogether indefinite and vague, and like the memory of a painful dream. Going towards the light, which I imagined proceeded from a physician's office, and which seemed to recede as I advanced, is the last glimmering recollection I can now recall. From that moment I was insensible. How long I remained in that condition—whether only that night, or many days and nights—I do not know; but when consciousness returned I found myself alone, in utter darkness, and in chains.

The pain in my head had subsided in a measure, but I was very faint and weak. I was sitting upon a low bench, made of rough boards, and without coat or hat. I was hand cuffed. Around my ankles also were a pair of heavy fetters. One end of a chain was fastened to a large ring in the floor, the other to the fetters on my ankles. I tried in vain to stand upon my feet. Waking from such a painful trance, it was some time before I could collect my thoughts. Where was I? What was the meaning of these chains? Where were Brown and Hamilton? What had I done to deserve imprisonment in such a dungeon? I could not comprehend. There was a blank of some indefinite period, preceding my awakening in that lonely place, the events of which the utmost stretch of memory was unable to recall. I listened intently for some sign or sound of life, but nothing broke the oppressive silence, save the clinking of my chains, whenever I chanced to move. I spoke aloud, but the sound of my voice startled me. I felt of my pockets, so far as the fetters would allow—far enough, indeed, to ascertain that I had not only been robbed of liberty, but that my money and free papers were also gone! Then did the idea begin to break upon my mind, at first dim and confused, that I had been kidnapped. But that I thought was incredible. There must have been some misapprehension—some unfortunate mistake. It could not be that a free citizen of New-York, who had wronged no man, nor violated any law, should be dealt with thus inhumanly. The more I contemplated my situation, however, the more I became confirmed in my suspicions. It was a desolate thought, indeed. I felt there was no trust or mercy in unfeeling man; and commending myself to the God of the oppressed, bowed my head upon my fettered hands, and wept most bitterly.

Chapter III

Some three hours elapsed, during which time I remained seated on the low bench, absorbed in painful meditations. At length I heard the crowing of a cock, and soon a distant rumbling sound, as of carriages hurrying through the streets, came to my ears, and I knew that it was day. No ray of light, however, penetrated my prison. Finally, I heard footsteps immediately overhead, as of some one walking to and fro. It occurred to me then that I must be in an underground apartment, and the damp, mouldy odors of the place confirmed the supposition. The noise above continued for at least an hour, when, at last, I heard footsteps approaching from without. A key rattled in the lock—a strong door swung back upon its hinges, admitting a flood of light, and two men entered and stood before me. One of them was a large, powerful man, forty years of age, perhaps, with dark, chestnut-colored hair, slightly interspersed with gray. His face was full, his complexion flush, his features grossly coarse, expressive of nothing but cruelty and cunning. He was about five feet ten inches high, of full habit, and, without prejudice, I must be allowed to say, was a man whose whole appearance was sinister and repugnant. His name was James H. Burch, as I learned afterwards—a well-known slave-dealer in Washington; and then, or lately connected in business, as a partner, with Theophilus Freeman, of New-Orleans. The person who accompanied him was a simple lackey, named Ebenezer Radburn, who acted merely in the capacity of turnkey. Both of these men still live in Washington, or did, at the time of my return through that city from slavery in January last.

The light admitted through the open door enabled me to observe the room in which I was confined. It was about twelve feet square—the walls of solid masonry. The floor was of heavy plank. There was one small window, crossed with great iron bars, with an outside shutter, securely fastened.

An iron-bound door led into an adjoining cell, or vault, wholly destitute of windows, or any means of admitting light. The furniture of the room in which I was, consisted of the wooden bench on which I sat, an old-fashioned, dirty box stove, and besides these, in either cell, there was neither bed, nor blanket, nor any

Burch was later arrested for his part in the kidnapping of Northup, but was almost immediately released for lack of evidence. He then had Northup arrested on a charge of 'collusion.' This charge, too, was dropped (*New York Times,* 19 Jan., 1853)

'January last' refers to January, 1853.

It was the viewing of these slave pens, which were at 8th and B SW, and so about a half mile from the Capitol, that made Henry Wilson (see page 53) an ardent abolitionist. They were owned and operated by William B. Williams, a notorious slave trader.

For another description of a slave pen, operated by Washington Robey, near the prison described by Northup, see Edward S. Abdy, *Journal of a Residence and Tour in the United States of North America, from April, 1833, to October, 1834, Volume 2*. London: Jon Murray, 1835.

other thing whatever. The door, through which Burch and Radburn entered, led through a small passage, up a flight of steps into a yard, surrounded by a brick wall ten or twelve feet high, immediately in rear of a building of the same width as itself. The yard extended rearward from the house about thirty feet. In one part of the wall there was a strongly ironed door, opening into a narrow, covered passage, leading along one side of the house into the street. The doom of the colored man, upon whom the door leading out of that narrow passage closed, was sealed. The top of the wall supported one end of a roof, which ascended inwards, forming a kind of open shed. Underneath the roof there was a crazy loft all round, where slaves, if so disposed, might sleep at night, or in inclement weather seek shelter from the storm. It was like a farmer's barnyard in most respects, save it was so constructed that the outside world could never see the human cattle that were herded there.

The building to which the yard was attached, was two stories high, fronting on one of the public streets of Washington. Its outside presented only the appearance of a quiet private residence. A stranger looking at it, would never have dreamed of its execrable uses. Strange as it may seem, within plain sight of this same house, looking down from its commanding height upon it, was the Capitol. The voices of patriotic representatives boasting of freedom and equality, and the rattling of the poor slave's chains, almost commingled. A slave pen within the very shadow of the Capitol!

Such is a correct description as it was in 1841, of Williams' slave pen in Washington, in one of the cellars of which I found myself so unaccountably confined.

"Well, my boy, how do you feel now?" said Burch, as he entered through the open door. I replied that I was sick, and inquired the cause of my imprisonment. He answered that I was his slave —that he had bought me, and that he was about to send me to New-Orleans. I asserted, aloud and boldly, that I was a freeman— a resident of Saratoga, where I had a wife and children, who were also free, and that my name was Northup. I complained bitterly of the strange treatment I had received, and threatened, upon my liberation, to have satisfaction for the wrong. He denied that I was free, and with an emphatic oath, declared that I came from Georgia. Again and again I asserted I was no man's slave, and insisted upon his taking off my chains at once. He endeavored to hush me, as if he feared my voice would be overheard. But I would not be silent, and denounced the authors of my imprisonment, whoever they might be, as unmitigated villains. Finding he could not quiet me, he flew into a towering passion. With blasphemous oaths, he called me a black liar, a runaway from Georgia, and every other profane and vulgar epithet that the most indecent fancy could conceive.

During this time Radburn was standing silently by. His business was, to oversee this human, or rather inhuman stable, receiving slaves, feeding, and whipping them, at the rate of two shillings a head per day. Turning to him, Burch ordered the paddle and cat-o'-ninetails to be brought in. He disappeared, and in a few moments returned with these instruments of torture. The paddle, as it is termed in slave-beating parlance, or at least the one with which I first became acquainted, and of which I now speak, was a piece of hard-wood board, eighteen or twenty inches long, moulded to the shape of an old-fashioned pudding stick, or ordinary oar The flattened portion, which was about the size in circumference of two open hands, was bored with a small auger in numerous places. The cat was a large rope of many strands—the strands unraveled, and a knot tied at the extremity of each.

As soon as these formidable whips appeared, I was seized by both of them, and roughly divested of my clothing. My feet, as has been stated, were fastened to the floor. Drawing me over the bench, face downwards, Radburn placed his heavy foot upon the fetters, between my wrists, holding them painfully to the floor. With the paddle, Burch commenced beating me. Blow after blow was inflicted upon my naked body. When his unrelenting arm grew tired, he stopped and asked if I still insisted I was a free man. I did insist upon it, and then the blows were renewed, faster and more energetically, if possible, than before. When again tired, he would repeat the same question, and receiving the same answer, continue his cruel labor. All this time, the incarnate devil was uttering most fiendish oaths. At length the paddle broke, leaving the useless handle in his hand. Still I would not yield. All his brutal blows could not force from my lips the foul lie that I was a slave. Casting madly on the floor the handle of the broken paddle, he seized the rope. This was far more painful than the other. I struggled with all my power, but it was in vain. I prayed for mercy, but my prayer was only answered with imprecations and with stripes. I thought I must die beneath the lashes of the accursed brute. Even now the flesh crawls upon my bones, as I recall the scene. I was all on fire. My sufferings I can compare to nothing else than the burning agonies of hell!

At last I became silent to his repeated questions. I would make no reply. In fact, I was becoming almost unable to speak. Still he plied the lash without stint upon my poor body, until it seemed that the lacerated flesh was stripped from my bones at every stroke. A man with a particle of mercy in his soul would not have beaten even a dog so cruelly. At length Radburn said that it was useless to whip me any more—that I would be sore enough. Thereupon Burch desisted, saying, with an admonitory shake of his fist in my face, and hissing the words through his firm-set teeth, that if ever I dared to utter again that I was entitled to my freedom, that I had been kidnapped, or any thing whatever of the kind, the castigation I had just received was nothing in comparison with what would follow. He swore that he would either conquer or kill me. With these consolatory words, the fetters were taken from my wrists, my feet still remaining fastened to the ring; the shutter of the little barred window, which had been opened, was again closed, and going out, locking the great door behind them, I was left in darkness as before.

In an hour, perhaps two, my heart leaped to my throat, as the key rattled in the door again. I, who had been so lonely, and who had longed so ardently to see some one, I cared not who, now shuddered at the thought of man's approach. A human face was fearful to me, especially a white one. Radburn entered, bringing with him, on a tin plate, a piece of shriveled fried pork, a slice of bread and a cup of water. He asked me how I felt, and remarked that I had received a pretty severe flogging. He remonstrated with me against the propriety of asserting my freedom. In rather a patronizing and confidential manner, he gave it to me as his advice, that the less I said on that subject the better it would be for me. The man evidently endeavored to appear kind—whether touched at the sight of my sad condition, or with the view of silencing, on my part, any further expression of my rights, it is not necessary now to conjecture. He unlocked the festers from my ankles, opened the shutters of the little window, and departed, leaving me again alone.

By this time I had become stiff and sore; my body was covered with blisters, and it was with great pain and difficulty that I could move. From the window I could observe nothing but the roof resting on the adjacent wall. At night I laid down upon the damp, hard floor, without any pillow or covering whatever. Punctually, twice a day, Radburn came in, with his pork, and bread, and water. I had but little appetite, though I was tormented with continual thirst. My wounds would not permit me to remain but a few minutes in any one position; so, sitting, or standing, or moving slowly round, I passed the days and nights. I was heart sick and discouraged. Thoughts of my family, of my wife and children, continually occupied my mind. When sleep overpowered me I dreamed of them—dreamed I was again in Saratoga—that I could see their faces, and hear their voices calling me. Awakening from the pleasant phantasms of sleep to the bitter realities around me, I could but groan and weep. Still my spirit was not broken. I indulged the anticipation of escape, and that speedily. It was impossible, I reasoned, that men could be so unjust as to detain me as a slave, when the truth of my case was known. Burch, ascertaining I was no runaway from Georgia, would certainly let me go. Though suspicions of Brown and Hamilton were not unfrequent, I could not reconcile myself to the idea that they were instrumental to my imprisonment. Surely they would seek me out —they would deliver me from thraldom. Alas! I had not then learned the measure of "man's inhumanity to man," nor to what limitless extent of wickedness he will go for the love of gain.

> This is a quote from Robert Burns's poem "Man was Made to Mourn: A Dirge" published in *Poems Chiefly in the Scottish Dialect*. Kilmarnock: John Wilson, 1786

In the course of several days the outer door was thrown open, allowing me the liberty of the yard. There I found three slaves— one of them a lad of ten years, the others young men of about twenty and twenty-five. I was not long in forming an acquaintance, and learning their names and the particulars of their history.

The eldest was a colored man named Clemens Ray. He had lived in Washington; had driven a hack, and worked in a livery stable there for a long time. He was very intelligent, and fully comprehended his situation. The thought of going south overwhelmed him with grief. Burch had purchased him a few days before, and had placed him there until such time as he was ready to send him to the New-Orleans market. From him I learned for the first time that I was in William's Slave Pen, a place I had never heard of previously. He described to me the uses for which it was designed. I repeated to him the particulars of my unhappy story, but he could only give me the consolation of his sympathy. He also advised me to be silent henceforth on the subject of my freedom for, knowing, the character of Burch, he assured me that it would only be attended with renewed whipping. The next eldest was named John Williams. He was raised in Virginia, not far from Washington. Burch had taken him in payment of a debt, and he constantly entertained the hope that his master would redeem him—a hope that was subsequently realized. The lad was a sprightly child, that answered to the name of Randall. Most of the time he was playing about the yard, but occasionally would cry, calling for his mother, and wondering when she would come. His mother's absence seemed to be the great and only grief in his little heart. He was too young to realize his condition, and when the memory of his mother was not in his mind, he amused us with his pleasant pranks.

At night, Ray, Williams, and the boy, slept in the loft of the shed, while I was locked in the cell. Finally we were each provided with blankets, such as are used upon horses—the only bedding I was allowed to have for twelve years afterwards. Ray and Williams asked me many questions about New-York—how colored people were treated there; how they could have homes and families of their own, with none to disturb and oppress them; and Ray, especially, sighed continually for freedom. Such conversations, however, were not in the hearing of Burch, or the keeper Radburn. Aspirations such as these would have brought down the lash upon our backs.

It is necessary in this narrative, in order to present a full and truthful statement of all the principal events in the history of my life, and to portray the institution of Slavery as I have seen and known it, to speak of well-known places, and of many persons who are yet living. I am, and always was, an entire stranger in Washington and its vicinity—aside from Burch and Radburn, knowing no man there, except as I have heard of them through my enslaved companions. What I am about to say, if false, can be easily contradicted.

I remained in Williams' slave pen about two weeks. The night previous to my departure a woman was brought in, weeping bitterly, and leading by the hand a little child. They were Randall's mother and half-sister. On meeting them he was overjoyed, clinging to her dress, kissing the child, and exhibiting every demonstration of delight. The mother also clasped him in her arms, embraced him tenderly, and gazed at him fondly through her tears, calling him by many an endearing name.

Emily, the child, was seven or eight years old, of light complexion, and with a face of admirable beauty. Her hair fell in curls around her neck, while the style and richness of her dress, and the neatness of her whole appearance indicated she had been brought up in the midst of wealth. She was a sweet child indeed. The woman also was arrayed in silk, with rings upon her fingers, and golden ornaments suspended from her ears. Her air and manners, the correctness and propriety of her language—all showed evidently, that she had sometime stood above the common level of a slave. She seemed to be amazed at finding herself in such a place as that. It was plainly a sudden and unexpected turn of fortune that had brought her there. Filling the air with her complaining she was hustled, with the children and myself, into the cell. Language can convey but an inadequate impression of the lamentations to which she gave incessant utterance. Throwing herself upon the floor, and encircling the children in her arms, she poured forth such touching words as only maternal love and kindness can suggest. They nestled closely to her, as if *there* only was there any safety or protection. At last they slept, their heads resting upon her lap. While they slumbered, she smoothed the hair back from their little foreheads, and talked to them all night long. She called them her darlings—her sweet babes—poor innocent things, that knew not the misery they were destined to endure. Soon they would have no mother to comfort them—they would be taken from her. What would become of them? Oh! she could not live away from her little Emmy and her dear boy. They had always been good children, and had such loving ways. It would break her heart, God knew, she said, if they were taken from her; and yet she knew they meant to sell them, and, may be, they would be separated, and could never see each other any more. It was enough to melt heart of stone to listen to the pitiful expressions of that desolate and distracted mother. Her name was Eliza; and this was the story of her life, as she afterwards related it:

She was the slave of Elisha Berry, a rich man, living in the neighborhood of Washington. She was born, I think she said, on his plantation. Years before, he had fallen into dissipated habits, and quarreled with his wife. In fact, soon after the birth of Randall, they separated. Leaving his wife and daughter in the house they had always occupied, he erected a new one nearby, on the estate. Into this house he brought Eliza; and, on condition of her living with him, she and her children were to be emancipated. She resided with him there nine years, with servants to attend upon her, and provided with every comfort and luxury of life. Emily was his child! Finally, her young mistress, who had always remained with her mother at the homestead, married a Mr. Jacob Brooks. At length, for some cause, (as I gathered from her relation,) beyond Berry's control, a division of his property was made. She and her children fell to the share of Mr. Brooks. During the nine years she had lived with Berry, in consequence of the position she was compelled to occupy, she and Emily had become the object of Mrs. Berry and her daughter's hatred and dislike. Berry himself she represented as a man of naturally a kind heart, who always promised her that she should have her freedom, and who, she had no doubt, would grant it to her then, if it were only in his power. As soon as they thus came into the possession and control of the daughter, it became very manifest they would not live long together. The sight of Eliza seemed to be odious to Mrs. Brooks; neither could she bear to look upon the child, half-sister, and beautiful as she was!

The day she was led into the pen, Brooks had brought her from the estate into the city, under pretence that the time had come when her free papers were to be executed, in fulfillment of her master's promise. Elated at the prospect of immediate liberty, she decked herself and little Emmy in their best apparel, and accompanied him with a joyful heart. On their arrival in the city, instead of being baptized into the family of freemen, she was delivered to the trader Burch. The paper that was executed was a bill of sale. The hope of years was blasted in a moment. From the hight of most exulting happiness to the utmost depths of wretchedness, she had that day descended. No wonder that she wept, and filled the pen with wailings and expressions of heart-rending woe.

The Red River is a tributary of the Mississippi river. It flows from West to East through northern Louisiana.

Eliza is now dead. Far up the Red River, where it pours its waters sluggishly through the unhealthy low lands of Louisiana, she rests in the grave at last—the only resting place of the poor slave! How all her fears were realized—how she mourned day and night, and never would be comforted—how, as she predicted, her heart did indeed break, with the burden of maternal sorrow, will be seen as the narrative proceeds.

Chapter IV

At intervals during the first night of Eliza's incarceration in the pen, she complained bitterly of Jacob Brooks, her young mistress' husband. She declared that had she been aware of the deception he intended to practice upon her, he never would have brought her there alive. They had chosen the opportunity of getting her away when Master Berry was absent from the plantation. He had always been kind to her. She wished that she could see him; but she knew that even he was unable now to rescue her. Then would she commence weeping again—kissing the sleeping children—talking first to one, then to the other, as they lay in their unconscious slumbers, with their heads upon her lap. So wore the long night away; and when the morning dawned, and night had come again, still she kept mourning on, and would not be consoled.

About midnight following, the cell door opened, and Burch and Radburn entered, with lanterns in their hands. Burch, with an oath, ordered us to roll up our blankets without delay, and get ready to go on board the boat. He swore we would be left unless we hurried fast. He aroused the children from their slumbers with a rough shake, and said they were d—d sleepy, it appeared. Going out into the yard, he called Clem Ray, ordering him to leave the loft and come into the cell, and bring his blanket with him. When Clem appeared, he placed us side by side, and fastened us together with hand-cuffs—my left hand to his right. John Williams had been taken out a day or two before, his master having redeemed him, greatly to his delight. Clem and I were ordered to march, Eliza and the children following, We were conducted into the yard, from thence into the covered passage, and up a flight of steps through a side door into the upper room, where I had heard the walking to and fro. Its furniture was a stove, a few old chairs, and a long table, covered with papers. It was a white-washed room, without any carpet on the floor, and seemed a sort of office. By one of the windows, I remember, hung a rusty sword, which attracted my attention. Burch's trunk was there. In obedience to his orders, I took hold of one of its handles with my unfettered hand, while he taking hold of the other, we proceeded out of the front door into the street in the same order as we had left the cell.

It was a dark night. All was quiet. I could see lights, or the reflection of them, over towards Pennsylvania Avenue, but there was no one, not even a straggler, to be seen. I was almost resolved to attempt to break away. Had I not been hand-cuffed the attempt would certainly have been made, whatever consequence might have followed. Radburn was in the rear, carrying a large stick, and hurrying up the children as fast as the little ones could walk. So we passed, hand-cuffed and in silence, through the streets of Washington through the Capital of a nation, whose theory of government, we are told, rests on the foundation of man's inalienable right to life, LIBERTY, and the pursuit of happiness! Hail! Columbia, happy land, indeed!

Reaching the steamboat, we were quickly hustled into the hold, among barrels and boxes of freight. A colored servant brought a light, the bell rung, and soon the vessel started down the Potomac, carrying us we knew not where. The bell tolled as we passed the tomb of Washington! Burch, no doubt, with uncovered head, bowed reverently before the sacred ashes of the man who devoted his illustrious life to the liberty of his country.

Northup was transferred in Richmond onto the Brig *Orleans*, bound for New Orleans. He was listed on the ship manifest as 'Plat Hamilton'

Scene in the Slave Pen At Washington, from Northup, *Twelve Years a Slave*. (from Docsouth collection)

Frontispiece engraving from *Personal Memoir of Daniel Drayton.* (from Library of Congress)

The Flight and Capture of the *Pearl*

Personal Memoir of Daniel Drayton
1855

While some abolitionists signed petitions and wrote newspapers, others took more direct action. The Underground Railroad, which had helped thousands escape to the North since its inception in 1810, is the best known example. Most people fleeing on the Underground Railroad walked all the way to freedom, hiding out in houses during the day. However, the largest single attempt came in 1848, when a Chesapeake waterman named Daniel Drayton tried to help 77 slaves escape from Washington DC by boat.

Drayton had for years traded goods up and down the eastern seaboard, sometimes as the owner of ships, sometimes as leaseholder of a ship. He was shipwrecked numerous times.

Once while running a hired boat from DC, he took on board a family of slaves and brought them to Frenchtown MD and freedom. Thereafter, having returned the boat to its owner and living with his family in Philadelphia, he was contacted by someone who requested that he travel back to DC and remove another family fearful of their being sold to the South. He finally convinced Captain Edward (or Edwin) Sayres of the *Pearl* to undertake the trip, and they set off for DC.

Their trip and its aftermath are described in this excerpt from Drayton's book.

Daniel Drayton was convicted of stealing slaves as well as transporting runaway slaves, while Sayres was at first exonerated. Drayton's conviction was overturned by the circuit court, leaving him facing heavy fines and court costs. Since Drayton was unable to come up with the money to pay the fines, he spent 4 years in jail until freed by Millard Fillmore after he had lost his bid for re-election.

This excerpt is from Daniel Drayton, *Personal Memoir of Daniel Drayton, for Four Years and Four Months a Prisoner (for Charity's Sake) in Washington Jail, Including a Narrative of the Voyage and Capture of the Schooner Pearl*, Boston: Bela Marsh, 1855.

For more on Frenchtown, see note on p. 45.

Captains Drayton and Sayres; or the Way in Which American are Treated, for Aiding the Cause of Liberty at Home, Philadelphia: Eastern Pennsylvania Anti-Slavery Society, 1848.

The slaves were, according to a letter written by John I. Slingerland on April 22, mainly sold down South by a Baltimore slave dealer.

Drayton's exploits, detailed in the newspapers of the day and discussed in Congress thereafter, and the public violence described therein, as well as his book, did much to bring the subject of slavery and abolition to the minds of the citizens of the northern states of the United States.

The narrative picks up where Drayton, Captain Sayres, and Chester English, the *Pearl*'s cook and sailor, have left Philadelphia and are making for Washington DC.

Presumably Upper Machodoc Creek, which is where the Dahlgren Naval Surface Warfare Center has been since 1918

Drayton landed at the 7th Street Wharf, at the corner of 7th and M streets SW

The *Union* was a pro-Buchanan and therefore pro-slavery paper. Henry S. Foote (1804–1880) was, in spite of being a Democratic Senator from Mississippi, strongly pro-Union.

We proceeded down the Delaware, and by the canal into the Chesapeake, making for the mouth of the Potomac. As we ascended that river we stopped at a place called Machudock, where I purchased, by way of cargo and cover to the voyage, twenty cords of wood; and with that freight on board we proceeded to Washington, where we arrived on the evening of Thursday, the 13th of April, 1848.

As it happened, we found that city in a great state of excitement on the subject of emancipation, liberty and the rights of man. A grand torch-light procession was on foot, in honor of the new French revolution, the expulsion of Louis-Philippe, and the establishment of a republic in France. Bonfires were blazing in the public squares, and a great out-door meeting was being held in front of the *Union* newspaper office, at which very enthusiastic and exciting speeches were delivered, principally by southern democratic members of Congress, which body was at that time in session. A full account of these proceedings, with reports of the speeches, was given in the *Union* of the next day. According to this report, Mr. Foote, the senator from Mississippi, extolled the French revolution as holding out "to the whole family of man a bright promise of the universal establishment of civil and religious liberty." He declared, in the same speech, "that the age of tyrants and of slavery was rapidly drawing to a close, and that the happy period to be signalized by the *universal emancipation* of man from the fetters of civic oppression, and the recognition in all countries of the great principles of popular sovereignty, equality and brotherhood, was at this moment visibly commencing." Mr. Stanton, of Tennessee, and others, spoke in a strain equally fervid and philanthropic. I am obliged to refer to the *Union* newspaper for an account of these speeches, as I did not hear them myself. I came to Washington, not to preach, nor to hear preached, emancipation, equality and brotherhood, but to put them into practice. Sayres and English went up to see the procession and hear the speeches. I had other things to attend to.

The news of my arrival soon spread among those who had been expecting it, though I neither saw nor had any direct communication with any of those who were to be my passengers. I had some difficulty in disposing of my wood, which was not a very first-rate article, but finally sold it, taking in payment the purchaser's note on sixty days, which I changed off for half cash and half provisions. As the trader to whom I passed the note had no hard bread, Sayres and myself went in the steamer to Alexandria to purchase a barrel,—a circumstance of which it was afterwards attempted to take advantage against us.

It was arranged that the passengers should come on board after dark on Saturday evening, and that we should sail about midnight. I had understood that the expedition, had principally originated in the desire to help off a certain family, consisting of a woman, nine children and two grand-children, who were believed to be legally entitled to their liberty. Their case had been in litigation for some time; but, although they had a very good case,—the lawyer whom they employed (Mr. Bradley, one of the most distinguished members of the bar of the district) testified, in the course of one of my trials, that he believed them to be legally free,—yet, as their money was nearly exhausted, and as there seemed to be no end to the law's delay and the pertinacity of the woman who claimed them, it was deemed best by their friends that they should get away if they could, lest she might seize them unawares, and sell them to some trader. In speaking of this case, the person with whom I communicated at Washington informed me that there were also quite a number of others who wished to avail themselves of this opportunity of escaping, and that the number of passengers was likely to be larger than had at first been calculated upon. To which I replied, that I did not stand about the number; that all who were on board before eleven o'clock I should take,—the others would have to remain behind.

Saturday evening, at supper, I let English a little into the secret of what I intended. I told him that the sort of ship-timber we were going to take would prove very easy to load and unload; that a number of colored people wished to take passage with us down the bay, and that, as Sayres and myself would be away the greater part of the evening, all he had to do was, as fast as they came on board, to lift up the hatch and let them pass into the hold, shutting the hatch down upon them. The vessel, which we had moved down the river since unloading the wood, lay at a rather lonely place, called White-house Wharf, from a whitish-colored building

Frederick Perry Stanton (1814–1894) was a Democratic Representative from Tennessee from 1845–1855.

For more information on the 'new French Revolution,' see p. 21.

Though there is no further evidence as to

which wharf is meant by this (no one else seems to have used the appellation 'White-house wharf') there is only one wharf shown on an 1853 plan of DC that fits Drayton's description. It is on 6th street, between N and O streets SW.

which stood upon it. The high bank of the river, under which a road passed, afforded a cover to the wharf, and there were only a few scattered buildings in the vicinity. Towards the town there stretched a wide extent of open fields. Anxious, as might naturally be expected, as to the result, I kept in the vicinity to watch the progress of events. There was another small vessel that lay across the head of the same wharf, but her crew were all black; and, going on board her just at dusk, I informed the skipper of my business, intimating to him, at the same time, that it would be a dangerous thing for him to betray me. He assured me that I need have no fears of him—that the other men would soon leave the vessel, not to return again till Monday, and that, for himself, he should go below and to sleep, so as neither to hear nor to see anything.

Shortly after dark the expected passengers began to arrive, coming stealthily across the fields, and gliding silently on board the vessel. I observed a man near a neighboring brick-kiln, who seemed to be watching them. I went towards him, and found him to be black. He told me that he understood what was going on, but that I need have no apprehension of him. Two white men, who walked along the road past the vessel, and who presently returned back the same way, occasioned me some alarm; but they seemed to have no suspicions of what was on foot, as I saw no more of them. I went on board the vessel several times in the course of the evening, and learned from English that the hold was fast filling up. I had promised him, in consideration of the unusual nature of the business we were engaged in, ten dollars as a gratuity, in addition to his wages.

Something past ten o'clock, I went on board, and directed English to cast off the fastenings and to get ready to make sail. Pretty soon Sayres came on board. It was a dead calm, and we were obliged to get the boat out to get the vessel's head round. After dropping down a half a mile or so, we encountered the tide making up the river; and, as there was still no wind, we were obliged to anchor. Here we lay in a dead calm till about daylight. The wind then began to breeze up lightly from the northward, when we got up the anchor and made sail. As the sun rose, we passed Alexandria. I then went into the hold for the first time, and there found my passengers pretty thickly stowed. I distributed bread among them, and knocked down the bulkhead between the hold and the cabin, in order that they might get into the cabin to cook. They consisted of men and women, in pretty equal proportions, with a number of boys and girls, and two small children. The wind kept increasing and hauling to the westward. Off Fort Washington we had to make two stretches, but the rest of the way we run before the wind.

Shortly after dinner, we passed the steamer from Baltimore for Washington, bound up. I thought the passengers on board took particular notice of us; but the number of vessels met with in a passage up the Potomac at that season is so few, as to make one, at least for the idle passengers of a steamboat, an object of some curiosity. Just before sunset, we passed a schooner loaded with plaster, bound up. As we approached the mouth of the Potomac, the wind hauled to the north, and blew with such stiffness as would make it impossible for us to go up the bay, according to our original plan. Under these circumstances, apprehending a pursuit from Washington, I urged Sayres to go to sea, with the intention of reaching the Delaware by the outside passage. But he objected that the vessel was not fit to go outside (which was true enough), and that the bargain was to go to Frenchtown. Having reached Point Lookout, at the mouth of the river, and not being able to persuade Sayres to go to sea, and the wind being dead in our teeth, and too strong to allow any attempt to ascend the bay, we came to anchor in Cornfield harbor, just under Point Lookout, a shelter usually sought by bay-craft encountering contrary winds when in that neighborhood.

We were all sleepy with being up all the night before, and, soon after dropping anchor, we all turned in. I knew nothing more till, waking suddenly, I heard the noise of a steamer blowing off steam alongside of us. I knew at once that we were taken. The black men came to the cabin, and asked if they should fight. I told them no; we had no arms, nor was there the least possibility of a successful resistance. The loud shouts and trampling of many feet overhead proved that our assailants were numerous. One of them lifted the hatch a little, and cried out, "Niggers, by G—d!" an exclamation to which the others responded with three cheers, and by banging the buts of their muskets against the deck. A lantern was called for, to read the name of the vessel; and it being ascertained to be the *Pearl*, a number of men came to the cabin-door, and called for Captain Drayton. I was in no great hurry to stir; but at length rose from my berth, saying that I considered myself their prisoner, and that I expected to be treated as such. While I was dressing, rather too slowly for the impatience of those outside, a sentinel, who had been stationed at the cabin-door, followed every motion of mine with his gun, which he kept pointed at me, in great apprehension, apparently, lest I should suddenly seize some dangerous weapon and make at him. As I came out of the cabin-door, two of them seized me, took me on board the steamer and tied me; and they did the same with Sayres and English, who were brought on board, one after the other. The

Frenchtown MD is just south of Elkton, MD at the head of the Elk River, a tributary of the Chesapeake Bay. It was the end of the line for a railroad that ran straight to New Castle, DE, and a travel book from 1840 describes one way of getting from Baltimore to Philadelphia is by taking a boat up the Elk River to Frenchtown, then the train to New Castle, then a boat from there to Philadelphia.

Point Lookout is the very tip of land in MD separating the Potomac from the Chesapeake Bay. Cornfield Harbor is just north thereof.

black people were left on board the *Pearl*, which the steamer took in tow, and then proceeded up the river.

To explain this sudden change in our situation, it is necessary to go back to Washington. Great was the consternation in several families of that city, on Sunday morning, to find no breakfast, and, what was worse, their servants missing. Nor was this disaster confined to Washington only. Georgetown came in for a considerable share of it, and even Alexandria, on the opposite side of the river, had not entirely escaped. The persons who had taken passage on board the *Pearl* had been held in bondage by no less than forty-one different persons. Great was the wonder at the sudden and simultaneous disappearance of so many "prime hands," roughly estimated, though probably with considerable exaggeration, as worth in the market not less than a hundred thousand dollars,—and all at "one fell swoop" too, as the District Attorney afterwards, in arguing the case against me, pathetically expressed it! There were a great many guesses and conjectures as to where these people had gone, and how they had gone; but it is very doubtful whether the losers would have got upon the right track, had it not been for the treachery of a colored hackman, who had been employed to carry down to the vessel two passengers who had been in hiding for some weeks previous, and who could not safely walk down, lest they might be met and recognized. Emulating the example of that large, and, in their own opinion at least, highly moral, religious and respectable class of white people, known as "dough-faces," this hackman thought it a fine opportunity to feather his nest by playing cat's-paw to the slave-holders. Seeing how much the information was in demand, and anticipating, no doubt, a large reward, he turned informer, and described the *Pearl* as the conveyance which the fugitives had taken; and, it being ascertained that the *Pearl* had actually sailed between Saturday night and Sunday morning, preparations were soon made to pursue her. A Mr. Dodge, of Georgetown, a wealthy old gentleman, originally from New England, missed three or four slaves from his family, and a small steamboat, of which he was the proprietor, was readily obtained. Thirty-five men, including a son or two of old Dodge, and several of those whose slaves were missing, volunteered to man her; and they set out about Sunday noon, armed to the teeth with guns, pistols, bowie-knives, &c., and well provided with brandy and other liquors. They heard of us on the passage down, from the Baltimore steamer and the vessel loaded with plaster. They reached the mouth of the river, and, not having found the *Pearl*, were about to return, as the steamer could not proceed into the bay without forfeiting her insurance. As a last chance, they looked into Cornfield harbor,

Several sources finger one Judson Digges (or Diggs) as the hackman, others mention a John Adams, who was paid a considerable sum of money by the owners thereafter, but no consensus exists.

The 1847 Webster's dictionary defines *doughfacism* as "the willingness to be led about by one of stronger mind and will."

where they found us, as I have related. This was about two o'clock in the morning. The *Pearl* had come to anchor about nine o'clock the previous evening. It is a hundred and forty miles from Washington to Cornfield harbor.

The steamer, with the *Pearl* in tow, crossed over from Point Lookout to Piney Point, on the south shore of the Potomac, and here the *Pearl* was left at anchor, a part of the steamer's company remaining to guard her, while the steamer, having myself and the other white prisoners on board, proceeded up Coan river for a supply of wood, having obtained which, she again, about noon of Monday, took the *Pearl* in tow and started for Washington.

The bearing, manner and aspect of the thirty-five armed persons by whom we had been thus seized and bound, without the slightest shadow of lawful authority, was sufficient to inspire a good deal of alarm. We had been lying quietly at anchor in a harbor of Maryland; and, although the owners of the slaves might have had a legal right to pursue and take them back, what warrant or authority had they for seizing us and our vessel? They could have brought none from the District of Columbia, whose officers had no jurisdiction or authority in Cornfield harbor; nor did they pretend to have any from the State of Maryland. Some of them showed a good deal of excitement, and evinced a disposition to proceed to lynch us at once. A man named Houver, who claimed as his property two of the boys passengers on board the *Pearl*, put me some questions in a very insolent tone; to which I replied, that I considered myself a prisoner, and did not wish to answer any questions; whereupon one of the bystanders, flourishing a dirk in my face, exclaimed, "If I was in his place, I'd put this through you!" At Piney Point, one of the company proposed to hang me up to the yard-arm, and make me confess; but the more influential of those on board were not ready for any such violence, though all were exceedingly anxious to get out of me the history of the expedition, and who my employers were. That I had employers, and persons of note too, was taken for granted on all hands; nor did I think it worth my while to contradict it, though I declined steadily to give any information on that point. Sayres and English very readily told all that they knew. English, especially, was in a great state of alarm, and cried most bitterly. I pitied him much, besides feeling some compunctions at getting him thus into difficulty; and, upon the representations which I made, that he came to Washington in perfect ignorance of the object of the expedition, he was finally untied. As Sayres was obliged to admit that he came to Washington to take away colored passengers, he was not regarded with so much favor. But it was evidently me whom they looked upon as the chief culprit, alone possessing a

The steamboat used was the *Salem*.

There is a Piney Point, MD just north of Point Lookout, it is above St. George Island, while the Coan River is due south thereof, in Virginia.

There are no Houvers in DC in 1852, several Hoovers, however. Who, exactly, this is is not clear.

knowledge of the history and origin of the expedition, which they were so anxious to unravel. They accordingly went to work very artfully to worm this secret out of me. I was placed in charge of one Orme, a police-officer of Georgetown, whose manner towards me was such as to inspire me with a certain confidence in him; who, as it afterwards appeared from his testimony on the trial, carefully took minutes—but, as it proved, very confused and incorrect ones—of all that I said, hoping thus to secure something that might turn out to my disadvantage. Another person, with whom I had a good deal of conversation, and who was afterwards produced as a witness against me, was William H. Craig, in my opinion a much more conscientious person than Orme, who seemed to think that it was part of his duty, as a police-officer, to testify to something, at all hazards, to help on a conviction. But this is a subject to which I shall have occasion to return presently.

In one particular, at least, the testimony of both these witnesses was correct enough. They both testified to my expressing pretty serious apprehensions of what the result to myself was likely to be. What the particular provisions were, in the District of Columbia, as to helping slaves to escape, I did not know; but I had heard that, in some of the slave-states, they were very severe; in fact, I was assured by Craig that I had committed the highest crime, next to murder, known in their laws. Under these circumstances, I made up my mind that the least penalty I should be apt to escape with was confinement in the penitentiary for life; and it is quite probable that I endeavored to console myself, as these witnesses testified, with the idea that, after all, it might, in a religious point of view, be all for the best, as I should thus be removed from temptation, and have ample time for reflection and repentance. But my apprehensions were by no means limited to what I might suffer under the forms of law. From the temper exhibited by some of my captors, and from the vindictive fury with which the idea of enabling the enslaved to regain their liberty was, I knew, generally regarded at the south, I apprehended more sudden and summary proceedings; and what happened afterwards at Washington proved that these apprehensions were not wholly unfounded. The idea of being torn in pieces by a furious mob was exceedingly disagreeable. Many men, who might not fear death, might yet not choose to meet it in that shape. I called to mind the apology of the Methodist minister, who, just after a declaration of his that he was not afraid to die, ran away from a furious bull that attacked him,—"that, though not fearing death, he did not like to be torn in pieces by a mad bull." I related this anecdote to Craig, and, as he testified on the trial, expressed my preference to be taken on the deck of the steamer and shot at

The 1852 directory of DC lists a J. H. Craig, police officer, living on 19th St NW, between G and H Streets.

once, rather than to be given up to a Washington mob to be baited and murdered. I talked pretty freely with Orme and Craig about myself, the circumstances under which I had undertaken this enterprise, my motives to it, my family, my past misfortunes, and the fate that probably awaited me; but they failed to extract from me, what they seemed chiefly to desire, any information which would implicate others. Orme told me, as he afterwards testified, that what the people in the District wanted was the principals; and that, if I would give information that would lead to them, the owners of the slaves would let me go, or sign a petition for my pardon. Craig also made various inquiries tending to the same point. Though I was firmly resolved not to yield in this particular, yet I was desirous to do all I could to soften the feeling against me; and it was doubtless this desire which led me to make the statements sworn to by Orme and Craig, that I had no connection with the persons called abolitionists,—which was true enough; that I had formerly refused large offers made me by slaves to carry them away; and that, in the present instance, I was employed by others, and was to be paid for my services.

On arriving off Fort Washington, the steamer anchored for the night, as the captors preferred to make their triumphant entry into the city by daylight. Sayres and myself were watched during the night by a regular guard of two men, armed with muskets, who were relieved from time to time. Before getting under weigh again,—which they did about seven o'clock in the morning of Tuesday, Feb. 18,—Sayres and myself were tied together arm-and-arm, and the black people also, two-and-two, with the other arm bound behind their backs. As we passed Alexandria, we were all ordered on deck, and exhibited to the mob collected on the wharves to get a sight of us, who signified their satisfaction by three cheers. When we landed at the steamboat-wharf in Washington, which is a mile and more from Pennsylvania Avenue, and in a remote part of the city, but few people had yet assembled. We were marched up in a long procession, Sayres and myself being placed at the head of it, guarded by a man on each side; English following next, and then the negroes. As we went along, the mob began to increase; and, as we passed Gannon's slave-pen, that slave-trader, armed with a knife, rushed out, and, with horrid imprecations, made a pass at me, which was very near finding its way through my body. Instead of being arrested, as he ought to have been, this slave-dealer was politely informed that I was in the hands of the law, to which he replied, "D—n the law! —I have three negroes, and I will give them all for one thrust at this d—d scoundrel!" and he followed along, waiting his opportunity to repeat the blow. The crowd, by this time, was

Fort Washington is a few miles due south of the southern tip of DC in Maryland.

This is presumably the same wharf that Drayton originally landed at, located at 7th and M streets SW.

greatly increased. We met an immense mob of several thousand persons coming down Four-and-a-half street, with the avowed intention of carrying us up before the capitol, and making an exhibition of us there. The noise and confusion was very great. It seemed as if the time for the lynching had come. When almost up to Pennsylvania Avenue, a rush was made upon us,—"Lynch them! lynch them! the d—n villains!" and other such cries, resounded on all sides. Those who had us in charge were greatly alarmed; and, seeing no other way to keep us from the hands of the mob, they procured a hack, and put Sayres and myself into it. The hack drove to the jail, the mob continuing to follow, repeating their shouts and threats. Several thousand people surrounded the jail, filling up the enclosure about it.

Our captors had become satisfied, from the statements made by Sayres and myself, and from his own statements and conduct, that the participation of English in the affair was not of a sort that required any punishment; and when the mob made the rush upon us, the persons having him in charge had let him go, with the intention that he should escape. After a while he had found his way back to the steamboat wharf; but the steamer was gone. Alone in a strange place, and not knowing what to do, he told his story to somebody whom he met, who put him in a hack and sent him up to the jail. It was a pity he lacked the enterprise to take care of himself when set at liberty, as it cost him four months' imprisonment and his friends some money. I ought to have mentioned before that, on arriving within the waters of the District, Sayres and myself had been examined before a justice of the peace, who was one of the captors; and who had acted as their leader. He had made out a commitment against us, but none against English; so that the persons who had him in charge were right enough in letting him go.

Sayres and myself were at first put into the same cell, but, towards night, we were separated. A person named Goddard, connected with the police, came to examine us. He went to Sayres first. He then came to me, when I told him that, as I supposed he had got the whole story out of Sayres, and as it was not best that two stories should be told, I would say nothing. Goddard then took from me my money. One of the keepers threw me in two thin blankets, and I was left to sleep as I could. The accommodations were not of the most luxurious kind. The cell had a stone floor, which, with the help of a blanket, was to serve also for a bed. There was neither chair, table, stool, nor any individual piece of furniture of any kind, except a night-bucket and a water-can. I was refused my overcoat and valise, and had nothing but my water-can to make a pillow of. With such a pillow, and the bare

John H. Goddard was a Justice of the Peace, and had been active in trying to retrieve the slaves who had left on the *Pearl*, in order to win the reward for their return.

stone floor for my bed, looked upon by all whom I saw with apparent abhorrence and terror,—as much so, to all appearance, as if I had been a murderer, or taken in some other desperate crime,—remembering the execrations which the mob had belched forth against me, and uncertain whether a person would be found to express the least sympathy for me (which might not, in the existing state of the public feeling, be safe), it may be imagined that my slumbers were not very sound.

Meanwhile the rage of the mob had taken, for the moment, another direction. I had heard it said, while we were coming up in the steamboat, that the abolition press must be stopped; and the mob accordingly, as the night came on, gathered about the office of the *National Era*, with threats to destroy it. Some little mischief was done; but the property-holders in the city, well aware how dependent Washington is upon the liberality of Congress, were unwilling that anything should occur to place the District in bad odor at the north. Some of them, also, it is but justice to believe, could not entirely give in to the slave-holding doctrine and practice of suppressing free discussion by force; and, by their efforts, seconded by a drenching storm of rain, that came on between nine and ten o'clock, the mob were persuaded to disperse for the present. The jail was guarded that night by a strong body of police, serious apprehensions being entertained, lest the mob, instigated by the violence of many southern members of Congress, should break in and lynch us. Great apprehension, also, seemed to be felt at the jail, lest we might be rescued; and we were subject, during the night, to frequent examinations, to see that all was safe. Great was the terror, as well as the rage, which the abolitionists appeared to inspire.

19th Century Chesapeake Bay schooner. Detail of print "The pirates attaching the police schooner *Julia Hamilton*," originally published in *Harper's Weekly*, March 1, 1884. (from Library of Congress)

Senator Henry Wilson (1812–1875) was a Senator from Massachusetts and 18th Vice-President of the United States. Wilson introduced the DC Emancipation Act into the Senate on December 16, 1861. Wilson, who was born Jeremiah Jones Colbath in New Hampshire, changed his name at age 21, moved to Massachusetts to become a shoemaker.

He was a member of the Massachusetts state legislature from 1841 until 1852, as well as owner and editor of the *Boston Republican*. Wilson was a Republican, although he was originally elected to the Senate by a coalition of Democrats, Free-Soilers, and Americans aka Know-Nothings. He spent much of his time as a Senator railing against the 'Slaveocray,' as the Slave Power was also known. Wilson went on to become the 18th Vice President of the United States, under Ulysses S. Grant. He died while in office on November 22, 1875, dying in the US Capitol. (from Library of Congress)

Bills Introduced

The Congressional Globe
December 16, 1861

In spite of the passing of the Fugitive Slave Act and the *Dred Scott* decision of 1857, the slave-owning states continued to feel that their rights were being curtailed, particularly by the election of Abraham Lincoln on November 6, 1860. The Slave Power, which had threatened to take over all branches of government, was in danger of collapsing.

A little over a month and a half after Lincoln's election, South Carolina voted to secede from the Union. They were followed by six other states by the time Abraham Lincoln took office on March 4, 1861. It did not take long for verbal hostilities to escalate to physical blows thereafter.

On December 16, 1861, almost exactly eight months after the Civil War had begun with the shelling of Fort Sumter, Senator Henry Wilson of Massachusetts introduced a bill entitled "A bill for the release of certain persons held to service or labor in the District of Columbia."

The following extract from the Congressional Globe for that date is the second item under the heading "Bills Introduced."

The *Daily National Intelligencer* printed the same information on December 17, and added the following: "This bill discharges all persons held to labor of African decent—the amount for each slave not to exceed three hundred dollars, and appropriates one million of dollars from the treasury."

The bill was 'taken from the table,' read a second time, given the appellation S. No. 108 and referred to the Committee on the District of Columbia on December 20 of that year.

"The Slave Power" was the collective name given to southern pro-slavery politicians and their northern enablers.

It was Wilson's desk that Richard Nixon used during his administration. Nixon had asked for 'Wilson's Desk' hoping to get the one Woodrow Wilson had used; instead, he was given Henry Wilson's

Mr. WILSON asked, and by unanimous consent obtained, leave to introduce a bill (S. No. 108) for the release of certain persons held to service or labor in the District of Columbia; which was read and passed to a second reading, and ordered to be printed.

Currier & Ives print from the 1872 presidential campaign showing Ulysses S. Grant and Henry Wilson. (from Library of Congress)

Joint Resolution of Instruction

Congressional Globe
April 2, 1862

On February 13, 1862, the Committee on the District of Columbia, having made some amendments to it, returned S. No. 108 to the full Senate. The bill was ordered to be printed. On February 27 of that year, Senator Wilson brought up the bill again, asking that it be discussed the next Wednesday, which would have been March 5. Instead, it was not until the 15th of March that the discussion began.

There followed several weeks of debates, the bill being brought up every few days for further emendation and discussion. During these discussions, several amendments were offered that dealt with the forcible emigration of freed slaves. One such amendment, offered by Rep. Saulsbury, stated that "the persons liberated under this act shall, within thirty days after the passage of the same, be removed, at the expense of the Federal Government, into the States of [the Union]; and that said persons shall be distributed to and among the said States, *pro rata*, according to the population of the same." This amendment ended up being voted down unanimously; even Rep. Saulsbury voted 'no.'

Other amendments dealt with emigration to Africa. At first, they were to be forcibly sent there, an amendment to the amendment simply gave the freed slaves the opportunity to emigrate, as well as authorizing some money for said emigration.

One attempt to derail the bill came from those governing the District of Columbia, the Common Council and the Board of Aldermen. It was signed only by the heads of these two councils as well as the current mayor of Washington, so it is uncertain as to how accurately this petition portrayed the general opinion of those living in the District of Columbia. At this time,

Congressional Globe, 37th Congress, 2nd Session, April 2, 1862.

For an excellent account of the discussions of the DC Emancipation Act, see Chapter 3 of Henry Wilson, *History of the Antislavery Measures of the Thirty-Seventh and Thirty-Eighth United-States Congresses, 1861-64.* Boston: Walker, Wise, and Company, 1864. The author is also the Senator who introduced S. No. 108.

Eric Foner.
*Reconstruc-
tion: Ameri-
ca's Unfin-
ished Busi-
ness.* New
York: Harper-
Collins, 2002.

however, both Council and Board as well as the Mayor
were elected by (white, male) citizens of the city, and
when, a few years later, these same voters had the
chance to vote on a referendum on enfranchisement,
there could be no doubt about the views of the voters:
"The result: 35 in favor of black suffrage, 6,951 against."
Others like to point out that in all of Georgetown, exactly
one voter cast his vote for enfranchisement.

In all, it seems that the views of the white citizens of
Washington DC in 1862 are well represented in the
following text.

MR. WRIGHT. I ask leave to present a memorial from the Board
of Aldermen of the city of Washington on this subject, and ask
that it be read.

The Secretary read it as follows:

IN BOARD OF ALDERMEN

Joint Resolution of Instruction

Be it resolved by the Board of Aldermen and Board of Common Council of the City of Washington, That these councils, dis-
claiming any desire improperly to interfere with the business of
the national Legislature, deem it not impertinent respectfully to
express the opinion that the sentiment of a large majority of the
people of this community is adverse to the unqualified abolition
of slavery in this District at the present critical juncture in our national affairs.

And be it further resolved, That the joint committee representing the interests of this corporation before Congress be, and are
hereby, instructed to urge respectfully upon the members of that
honorable body, as the constitutional guardians of the interests
and rights of the people of this District, the expediency and the
justice of so shaping any legislation affecting the African race
here as to provide just and proper safe-guards against converting
this city, located as it is between two slaveholding States, into an
asylum for free negroes–a population undesirable in every American community, and which it has been deemed necessary to exclude altogether from some even of the non-slaveholding States.

Z. RICHARDS
President of the Board of Common Council.
W. T. DOVE
President of the Board of Aldermen.

Approved: RICHARD WALLACH,
Mayor.

Slavery in the District of Columbia

Daily National Intelligencer
April 4, 1862

Finally, on April 3, 1862, S. 108 was brought up one more time, was voted on, and passed. The *Daily National Intelligencer* reported the next day the scene in the Senate.

Slavery in the District of Columbia

The Senate resumed the consideration of the bill for the release of persons held to service or labor in the District of Columbia, and the debate, which had occupied several days past, was continued by Mr. McDOUGALL, Mr. TEN EYCK, Mr. POWELL, Mr. BAYARD, and others.

Then the various propositions to modify the message, by providing amongst other things for gradual emancipation, were disposed of, and the bill was passed with but slight modifications from its original shape, as heretofore published, and those but amendments giving greater security to the emancipated slave, by establishing a registration of freedom, providing for the admissibility of testimony without regard to color, requiring claimants to embody in their petitions a statement of their loyalty, and that they have not been in arms against the Government or given aid and comfort to the enemies. Such a provision compels the claimants to swear to their fidelity to the Government, as the petition must be under oath, but even then it is not to be deemed to be evidence of the fact sworn to. It will require an oath as to loyalty before compensation can be received, but the Commissioners may receive evidence to contradict that averment.

The vote on the passage of the bill was as follows:

YEAS—Messrs. Browning, Chandler, Clark, Collaber,

Senator James A. McDougall (1817–1867) was Senator from California from 1861–1867. Although a Democrat, he was elected as an anti-secessionist

John Ten Eyck (1814–1879) represented New Jersey from 1859–1865 as a member of the Republican party.

Lazarus Powell (1812–1867) of Kentucky, served one term in the Senate 1859–1865. He was in frequent conflict with Lincoln over the suspension of habeas corpus as well as other issues of states's rights.

James Bayard jr, Democrat from Delaware, served from 1851–1864, when he resigned in order to avoid signing an oath of loyalty to the Union. On the death of his successor, he retook the seat in 1867 and served until 1869

The Wilson voting against the bill should be 'Wilson of Missouri' Robert Wilson was Senator from 1862–1863 as a member of the Unionist party

Dixon, Doolittle, Fessenden, Foot, Foster, Grimes, Harlan, Harris, Howard, Howe, King, Lane of Indiana, Morril, Pomeroy, Sherman, Sumner, Ten Eyck, Trumon, Wade, Wilkinson, Wilmot, and Wilson of Massachusetts.—29

NAYS—Messrs. Bayard, Carlile, Davis, Henderson, Kennedy, Latham, McDougall, Nesmith, Powell, Saulsbury, Stark, Willey, Wilson of Massachusetts [sic], and Wright—14.

The District business, which was the special order for to-day, will occupy the attention of the Senate to-morrow.

After passing the emancipation bill, the Senate adjourned, amidst an outburst of applause in the gallery.

SLAVERY IN THE DISTRICT OF COLUMBIA.

The Senate resumed the consideration of the bill for the release of persons held to service or labor in the District of Columbia, and the debate, which has occupied several days past, was continued by Mr. McDOUGALL, Mr. TEN EYCK, Mr. POWELL, Mr. BAYARD, and others.

Then the various propositions to modify the measure, by providing amongst other things for gradual emancipation, were disposed of, and the bill was passed with but slight modification from its original shape, as heretofore published, and those but amendments giving greater security to the emancipated slave, by establishing a registration of freedom, providing for the admissibility of testimony without regard to color, requiring claimants to embody in their petitions a statement of their loyalty, and that they have not been in arms against the Government or given aid and comfort to its enemies. Such a provision compels the claimants to swear to their fidelity to the Government, as the petition must be under oath, but even then it is not to be deemed to be evidence of the fact sworn to. It will require an oath as to loyalty before compensation can be received, but the Commissioners may receive evidence to contradict that averment.

The vote on the passage of the bill was as follows:

YEAS—Messrs. Browning, Chandler, Clark, Collamer, Dixon, Doolittle, Fessenden, Foot, Foster, Grimes, Harlan, Harris, Howard, Howe, King, Lane of Indiana, Morrill, Pomeroy, Sherman, Sumner, Ten Eyck, Trumbull, Wade, Wilkinson, Wilmot, and Wilson of Massachusetts—29

NAYS—Messrs. Bayard, Carlile, Davis, Henderson, Kennedy, Latham, McDougall, Nesmith, Powell, Saulsbury, Stark, Willey, Wilson of Massachusetts, and Wright—14

The District business, which was the special order for to-day, will occupy the attention of the Senate to-morrow.

After passing the emancipation bill the Senate adjourned amidst an outburst of applause in the galleries.

Image of the above article as printed in the *Daily National Intelligencer.* April 4, 1862 (from DC Public Library)

Emancipation in the District– Mr. Lincoln's Opinions.

New York Times Editorial
April 15, 1862

Following passage of S. No. 108 by the Senate, the House of Representatives began its part of the process, having received the bill on April 7, 1862. A call for it to be rejected was voted down and, as it required a appropriation, it was passed on to the Committee of the Whole on the state of the Union.

Debate proper began on April 10, 1862, and continued the next day interrupted only by the occasional message from the Senate, in which they were informed that the Senate had passed some piece of legislation. The main point of discussion of those opposing the bill was that slavery was, in their minds, in the process of eliminating itself in the District, and that there was no need to hurry the situation. The counter argument was, of course, that this bill was about more than the slaves thus freed but instead, according to Representative John Bingham of Ohio, illustrated "the great principle that this day shakes the throne of every despot upon the globe; and that is, whether man was made for government, or government made for man." On the evening of April 11, it was passed by a vote of 92 to 38.

On April 14, the House signed the bill in the same form as that sent to them by the Senate, sending the bill to the President for signature.

The following piece ran in the *New York Times* of April 15, 1862, the day after Lincoln had received the bill from Congress. The article later ran in the *National Daily Intelligencer* of April 17, 1862, directly below the news that Lincoln had, indeed, signed the bill.

The House Committee of the Whole on the state of the Union is a committee that is called whenever questions of "tax or charge on the people, raising revenue, directly or indirectly making appropriations of money or property or requiring such appropriations to be made, authorizing payments out of appropriations already made, releasing any liability to the United States for money or property, or referring a claim to the Court of Claims" (as per House Rule 18) are before the House.

Emancipation in the District—Mr. Lincoln's Opinions.

The bill manumitting the slaves in the District of Columbia reached the President yesterday. If it is to become a law, it will, no doubt, be returned with approval to-day; awhile its retention will justify a belief that it is to go back to the other end of the avenue with a veto in company. Those who are best acquainted with the views of the President, give confident assurances of the executive sanction; asserting that MR. LINCOLN's approbation would have been cordial had the measure been a little less hasty and radical, but that he does not care to take the responsibility of vetoing an act of Congress on other than constitutional grounds.

I may aid in fathoming MR. LINCOLN's opinions in the matter, to recall a page or two of his political biography. When in the Illinois Legislature, in 1837, resolutions strongly Pro-Slavery, were passed almost unanimously, the exceptions to unanimity were DANIEL STONE and ABRAHAM LINCOLN, members from Sangamon County. The following passage was contained in a protest entered on the minutes, and signed by those two members: "The congress of the United States has the power, under the Constitution, to abolish Slavery in the District of Columbia; but that the power ought not to be exercised *unless at the request of the people of said District.*"

On the 13th of December, 1848, MR. PALFREY of Massachusetts, asked leave to introduce to the House of Representatives, a bill repealing all laws sustaining Slavery in the District, MR. LINCOLN, then a member from Illinois, objected, "not believing in the expediency of abolishing Slavery in the District *without compensation to slaveowners.*"

On the 16th of January 1849, MR. LINCOLN introduced into the House a bill providing for the abolition of Slavery in the District, in which the principle of full compensation was reserved; and the right of the inhabitants to vote upon the measure was asserted in the following section:

"SECTION 6. That the elective officers, within said District of Columbia, are empowered and required to open polls at all the usual places of holding elections, on the first Monday of April next, and receive the vote of every free white male citizen above the age of twenty-one years, having resided within said District for the period of one year or more next preceding the time of such voting for or against this act, to proceed in taking said votes in all respects herein not specified, as at elections under the municipal laws, and with as little delay as possible, to transmit correct statements of the votes so cast to the

The text of this resolution as well as Lincoln and Stone's protest can be seen on the opposite page.

See page 22 for the complete text of the bill Lincoln attempted to introduce that day.

Lincoln, on March 14, 1862, had written a letter to Senator McDougall in which he showed that the cost of compensated emancipation

President of the United States; and it shall be the duty of the President to canvass said votes immediately, *and if a majority of them be found to be for this act, to forthwith issue his proclamation, giving notice of the fact, and this act shall only be in full force and effect on and after the day of such proclamation.*"

To pursue the inquiry to the present time, we have only to interrogate the recent message upon emancipation in the the the Border States, to learn that the President not only retains his convictions as to compensation and the propriety of consulting the will of communities retaining the institution, but thinks that the liberation should be gradual, and attended with ample arrangements for colonization. The bill now lying before him or signature provides indemnity to owners, and means to colonize the blacks. It omits to consult the will of the people of the District, and makes the liberation immediate; two important points in which the view of the President are disregarded. The probability is, the divergency is not so serious as to influence MR. LINCOLN to defeat the bill.

for five border states (including DC) was less than that the cost of running the war for 87 days. This can be seen on p. 144, at the end of this book.

The Illinois Assembly joined in the general disapproval, and on March 3d passed the following resolutions:

" Resolved by the General Assembly of the State of Illinois :
" That we highly disapprove of the formation of Abolition societies, and of the doctrines promulgated by them.
" That the right of property in slaves is sacred to the slave-holding States by the Federal Constitution, and that they cannot be deprived of that right without their consent.
" That the General Government cannot abolish slavery in the District of Columbia against the consent of the citizens of said District, without a manifest breach of good faith.
" That the Governor be requested to transmit to the States of Virginia, Alabama, Mississippi, New York, and Connecticut a copy of the foregoing report and resolutions."

Lincoln refused to vote for these resolutions. In his judgment no expression on the slavery question should go unaccompanied by the statement that it was an evil, and he had the boldness to protest immediately against the action of the House. He found only one man in the Assembly willing to join him in his action. These two names are joined to the document they presented:

" Resolutions upon the subject of domestic slavery having passed both branches of the General Assembly at its present session, the undersigned hereby protest against the passage of the same.
" They believe that the institution of slavery is founded on both injustice and bad policy, but that the promulgation of abolition doctrines tends rather to increase than abate its evils.
" They believe that the Congress of the United States has no power under the Constitution to interfere with the institution of slavery in the different States.
" They believe that the Congress of the United States has power under the Constitution to abolish slavery in the District of Columbia, but that the power ought not to be exercised unless at the request of the people of the District.
" The difference between these opinions and those contained in the above resolutions, is their reason for entering this protest. " DAN STONE,
" A. LINCOLN,
" Representatives from the County of Sangamon."

Detail of an article in *McClure's Magazine* showing both the 1837 Illinois resolution and the text of Lincoln and Stone's protests thereto. From Ida M. Tarbell, "Abraham Lincoln" *McClure's Magazine*, 6.4, March 1896. (From University of Michigan Library, via Google Books)

S. 108.

IN THE SENATE OF THE UNITED STATES.

MARCH 12, 1862.

Printed as amended and proposed to be amended.

A BILL

For the release of certain persons held to service or labor in the District of Columbia.

1   *Be it enacted by the Senate and House of Representa-*

2 *tives of the United States of America in Congress assembled,*

3 That all persons held to service or labor within the District of

4 Columbia, by reason of African descent, are hereby discharged

5 and freed of and from all claim to such service or labor; and

6 from and after the passage of this act neither slavery nor in-

7 voluntary servitude, except for crime, whereof the party shall

8 be duly convicted, shall hereafter exist in said District.

1   SEC. 2. *And be it further enacted,* That all persons loyal

2 to the United States holding claims to service or labor against

3 persons discharged therefrom by this act may, within ninety

4 days from the passage thereof, but not thereafter, present to

5 the commissioners hereinafter mentioned their respective

An Act For the Release of Certain Persons Held to Service or Labor in the District of Columbia

Bill as signed by President Lincoln
April 16, 1862

The bill as signed by Abraham Lincoln on April 16, 1862, was unique in that it was the first (and, in the end, only) time that the owners of slaves were to be compensated. Furthermore, the bill uses neither the word 'slave' nor 'emancipation.'

The bill allowed for for an average of $300 for each slave, as well as giving each freed person the right to emigrate to Africa as well as $100 dollars to help in their emigration, providing for $100,000 to this end.

In order to make sure the resolutions of the bill were put into effect, a commission was to be appointed to see through the freeing of the slaves and the compensation of their former masters—as long as they were loyal to the United States.

Illustration on opposite page shows first page of the bill as printed. (from Library of Congress)

Thirty-Seventh Congress of the United States of America;
At the Second Session
Begun and held at the city of Washington, on Monday the -second- day of December, one thousand eight hundred and sixty-one
AN ACT
For the release of certain persons held to service or labor in the District of Columbia

Be it enacted by the Senate and House of Representatives of the United States of America in Congress assembled, That all persons held to service or labor within the District of Columbia by reason of African descent are hereby discharged and freed of and from all claim to such service or labor; and from and after the passage of this act neither slavery nor involuntary servitude, except for crime, whereof the party shall be duly convicted, shall hereafter exist in said District.

Sec. 2. *And be it further enacted,* That all persons loyal to the United States, holding claims to service or labor against persons discharged therefrom by this act, may, within ninety days from the passage thereof, but not thereafter, present to the commissioners hereinafter mentioned their respective statements or petitions in writing, verified by oath or affirmation, setting forth the names, ages, and personal description of such persons, the manner in which said petitioners acquired such claim, and any facts touching the value thereof, and declaring his allegiance to the Government of the United States, and that he has not borne arms against the United States during the present rebellion, nor in any way given aid or comfort thereto: *Provided,* That the oath of the party to the petition shall not be evidence of the facts therein stated.

Sec. 3. *And be it further enacted,* That the President of the United States, with the advice and consent of the Senate, shall appoint three commissioners, residents of the District of Columbia, any two of whom shall have power to act, who shall receive the petitions above mentioned, and who shall investigate and determine the validity and value of the claims therein presented, as aforesaid, and appraise and apportion, under the proviso hereto annexed, the value in money of the several claims by them found to be valid: *Provided, however,* That the entire sum so appraised and apportioned shall not exceed in the aggregate an amount equal to three hundred dollars for each person shown to have been so held by lawful claim: *And provided, further,* That no claim shall be allowed for any slave or slaves brought into said District after the passage of this act, nor for any slave claimed by any person who has borne arms against the Government of the United States in the present rebellion, or in any way given aid or comfort thereto, or which originates in or by virtue of any transfer heretofore made, or which shall hereafter be made by any person who has in any manner aided or sustained the rebellion against the Government of the United States.

There had been a long-standing attempt to return freed slaves to Africa by the American Colonization Society. Their work was supported by Lincoln, though he later reversed his opinion.

[Sections 4-6, which deal with the how the committees are to be run, are omitted. –ed]

Sec. 7. *And be it further enacted,* That for the purpose of carrying this act into effect there is hereby appropriated, out of any money in the Treasury not otherwise appropriated, a sum not exceeding one million of dollars.

Sec. 8. *And be it further enacted*, That any person or persons who shall kidnap, or in any manner transport or procure to be taken out of said District, any person or persons discharged and freed by the provisions of this act, or any free person or persons with intent to re-enslave or sell such person or person into slavery, or shall re-enslave any of said freed persons, the person of persons so offending shall be deemed guilty of a felony, and on conviction thereof in any court of competent jurisdiction in said District, shall be imprisoned in the penitentiary not less than five nor more that twenty years.

Sec. 9. *And be it further enacted*, That within twenty days, or within such further time as the commissioners herein provided for shall limit, after the passage of this act, a statement in writing or schedule shall be filed with the clerk of the Circuit court for the District of Columbia, by the several owners or claimants to the services of the persons made free or manumitted by this act, setting forth the names, ages, sex, and particular description of such persons, severally; and the said clerk shall receive and record, in a book by him to be provided and kept for that purpose, the said statements or schedules on receiving fifty cents each therefor, and no claim shall be allowed to any claimant or owner who shall neglect this requirement.

Sec. 10. *And be it further enacted*, That the said clerk and his successors in office shall, from time to time, on demand, and on receiving twenty-five cents therefor, prepare, sign, and deliver to each person made free or manumitted by this act, a certificate under the seal of said court, setting out the name, age, and description of such person, and stating that such person was duly manumitted and set free by this act.

Sec. 11. *And be it further enacted*, That the sum of one hundred thousand dollars, out of any money in the Treasury not otherwise appropriated, is hereby appropriated, to be expended under the direction of the President of the United States, to aid in the colonization and settlement of such free persons of African descent now residing in said District, including those to be liberated by this act, as may desire to emigrate to the Republics of Hayti or Liberia, or such other country beyond the limits of the United States as the President may determine: *Provided*, The expenditure for this purpose shall not exceed one hundred dollars for each emigrant.

Sec. 12. *And be it further enacted*, That all acts of Congress and all laws of the State of Maryland in force in said District, and all

The convoluted terminology used in section 12 was necessary because, at this time, Washington DC did not have a full set of laws, but rather a hodgepodge of laws inherited from Maryland as well as some passed in the District itself. Although there were multiple attempts to remedy this state of affairs, it was only at the beginning of the 20th Century that, finally, the District of Columbia was given a complete set of laws.

ordinances of the cities of Washington and Georgetown, inconsistent with the provisions of this act, are hereby repealed.

Galusha A. Grow
Speaker of the House of Representatives

Solomon Foot
President of the Senate pro tempore

Approved, April 16, 1862.   Abraham Lincoln

For more on
Galusha Grow
and Solomon
Foot, see p. 71

Signatures at bottom of the District of Columbia Emancipation Act. The three signatures are, from the top, Galusha A. Grow, Speaker of the House of Representatives, Solomon Foot, President of the Senate *pro tempore*, and Abraham Lincoln. (from DC Office of the Secretary.)

Emancipation in This District

Daily National Intelligencer
April 17, 1862

The *Daily National Intelligencer* published this brief
article on the day after Lincoln had affixed his signature
to the DC Emancipation Act. Just below it was the
article (which can be seen on page 60) copied from the
New York Times. The *Intelligencer* shortened the title to
"Opinions of Mr. Lincoln" but also added a long exegesis
on the subject by the Hon. W. McKee Dunn, in which
Dunn (who had voted for the bill) showed that he was
entirely for emancipation, but was not willing to do
anything about it, as well as the full text of the act. The
Dunn text is interesting only in the the the *Intelligencer*
changed a few words to make Dunn look even less pro-
emancipation than he really was.

The rival *Evening Star,* on the other hand, mentioned
the event only in passing, in the middle of the daily
congressional update: "The message of the President,
announcing his approval of the bill abolishing slavery in
the District, was read."

EMANCIPATION IN THE DISTRICT

Our readers will find in a preceding column of this day's paper an official copy of the act of Congress abolishing slavery in
the District of Columbia. The bill was signed by the President
yesterday, and returned to Congress accompanied by a special
message from the President in the following words:

Fellow-citizens of the Senate
and the House of Representatives:
The act entitled "An act for the release of certain persons held
to service or labor in the District of Columbia" has this day been
approved and signed.

I have never doubted the constitutional authority of Congress to abolish slavery in this District, and I have ever desired to see the national capital freed from the institution in some satisfactory way. Hence there has never been, in my mind, any question upon the subject except the one of expediency, arising in view of all the circumstances. If there be matters within and about this not which might have taken a course or shaper more satisfactory to my judgment, I do not attempt to specify them. I am gratified that the two principles of compensation and colonization are both recognized and practically applied in the act.

In the matter of compensation it is provided that claims may be presented within ninety days from the passage of the act, "but not thereafter," and there is no saving for minors, femmes-covert, insane, or absent persons. I presume that this is an omission by mere oversight, and I recommend that it be supplied by an amendatory or supplemental act.   ABRAHAM LINCOLN
April 16, 1862

Image of above article as printed in the *Daily National Intelligencer* on April 17, 1862 (from DC Public Library)

An Act Supplementary to the "Act for the Release of Certain Persons Held to Service or Labor in the District of Columbia" Approved April Sixteen, Eighteen Hundred and Sixty-two

Signed by President Lincoln
July 12, 1862

> Just under three months after having signed the DC emancipation act, Lincoln signed a supplementary act to it. The additions to it were, in general, minor, allowing more flexibility in the taking of oaths about the ownership of slaves, however the final section, added just before the bill passed the Senate on July 7, 1862, said that "in all judicial proceedings in the District of Columbia there shall be no exclusion of any witness on account of color."

Thirty-Seventh Congress of the United States of America;
At the Second Session
Begun and held at the city of Washington, the Second day of December, one thousand eight hundred and sixty-one
An Act
Supplementary to the "Act for the release of certain persons held to service or labor in the District of Columbia," approved April sixteen; eighteen hundred and sixty-two.

Be it enacted by the Senate and House of Representatives of the United States of America in Congress assembled, That the oath or affirmation required by the second section of the act entitled "An act for the release of certain persons held to service or labor in the District of Columbia," to verify the statements or petitions in writing filed before the commissioners, under the act aforesaid, of persons holding claim to service or labor against persons of African descent, freed and discharged therefrom, under the act aforesaid, may in all cases in which the persons holding claims, as aforesaid, are infants or minors, be made by the guardian or by any other person, whether separately or jointly, having the custody, management, or control by law of the person and property of such infants or minors; and that in all cases in which the persons holding claims as aforesaid are non-residents of the District of Columbia, or resident absentees, the oath or affirmation required as aforesaid may be made by the attorney or agent of said non-resident or resident absentees; and in all cases in which the statements or petitions, required as aforesaid, of persons in the military or naval service of the United States, shall have been or may be hereafter verified before any commander of any military post, or of any officer having a separate command of any military force in the field, or before any captain, commander, or lieutenant commanding in the navy, the same shall be received and deemed valid, to all intents and purposes, as fully as if the verification had been or were made before any officer competent by law to take and administer oaths and affirmations: Provided, That the commissioners shall be satisfied that, at the time of the verification aforesaid, the person making the same was employed in the military or naval service of the United States within the jurisdiction of a rebellious State or Territory, and unable to make the oath or affirmation required, as aforesaid, before any officer authorized by law to take or administer the same, holding allegiance to the United States.

Sec. 2. And be it further enacted, That if any person, having claim, to the service or labor of any person or persons in the District of Columbia by reason of African descent, shall neglect or refuse to file with the clerk of the circuit court of the District of Columbia the statement in writing, or schedule provided in the ninth section of the act approved April sixteen, eighteen hundred and sixty-two, to which this is supplementary, then it shall be lawful for the person or persons, whose services are claimed as aforesaid, to file such statement in writing or schedule setting forth the particular facts mentioned in said ninth section; and the said clerk shall receive and record the same as provided in said section on receiving fifty cents each therefor.

Sec 3. And be it further enacted, That whenever the facts set forth in the said statement or schedule shall be found by the commissioners to be true, the said clerk and his successors in office shall prepares, sign, and deliver certificates, as prescribed in the tenth section, of the act to which this is supplementary, to such person or persons as shall file their statements in pursuance of the foregoing section, in all respects the same as if such statements were filed by the person having claim to their service or labor.

Sec. 4. And be it farther enacted, That all persons held to service or labor under the laws of any State, and who at any time since the sixteenth day of April, anno Domini eighteen hundred and sixty-two, by the consent of the person to whom such service or labor is claimed to be owing, have been actually employed within the District of Columbia, or also shall be hereafter thus employed, are hereby declared free, and forever released from such servitude, anything in the laws of the United States or of any State to the contrary notwithstanding.

Sec. 5. And be it further enacted, That in all judicial proceedings in the District of Columbia there shall be no exclusion of any witness on account of color.

Galusha A. Grow
Speaker of the House of Representatives

Solomon Foot
President of the Senate pro tempore

Approved July 12, 1862   Abraham Lincoln

certify that this act
did originate in the Senate
J. W. Forney
Secretary

Galusha Aaron Grow (1822–1907) was a Representative from Pennsylvania, serving from 1851 until 1863, then from 1894 until 1903. He was speaker of the House from 1861 until 1863, and was the last Speaker who lost his re-election until Tom Foley lost his seat in 1994.

Solomon Foot (1802–1866) was a Senator from Vermont from 1841 until 1866, and the President *pro tempore* of the Senate from 1861 until 1864.

John Weiss Forney (1817–1881) was a newspaper editor who was Clerk of the House of Representatives from 1851 to 1856, and 1860 to 1861, then secretary of the Senate from 1861 until 1868.

Galusha Grow and Solomon Foot (from Library of Congress)

Date of Filing. 1862.	Docket Number.	NAMES OF PETITIONERS.	No.	Names.	Claimants.	Assessors.	Commission.	REMARKS.
May 26	454	Lucy E. Mattingly	1	Leonard	1600	1250	1250	$547.50
" "	455	Ann Emelia Ward	1	Cecelia Thomas	1000	1200	1200	525.60
" "	456	Ulysses Ward	2	Rachel Cole	800	500	800	354.40
				Jene Cole	100	300		Noach
" "	457	Anthony Addison	7	Samuel Mulliken		200		87.60
				Elizabeth Bruce		200		87.60
				Lizzie Lewis				306.60
				Marion Lewis	2000	1400	1500	175.20	657.00
				Mary Solomon		700		306.60
				Thomas Solomon		600		279.	Pay $551.60
				Julia Solomon		500	1700	219.
" "	458	Louisa G. Beall	2	Betty Harris	300	200		87.60
				Josephine Harris	900	1200	1300	481.80
" "	459	Benjamin S. Bohrer	13	Arabella Nash	900	1000		438.
				Martha Nash	700	1200		525.60
				Archy Nash	800	1300		569.40
				Horace Nash	700	900		394.20
				Adelaide Nash	700	950		416.10
				Maud Infant		50		21.90
				George Ruffin Nash	800	900		394.20
				James Nash	800	700		306.60
				Selema Nash	600	800		350.40
				George Green	1200	1300		569.40
				Alexander Green	800	1000		657.
				John Green	700	1300		569.40
				William Marye	800	1300	1200	569.40	$7147.60
" "	460	Betty Robinson (Colored)	1	John Robinson	1000	1400	1400	613.20
May 27	461	Sarah E. King	6	Mary Chase	100	150		65.70
				Rachel Coquire	600	1000		438.
				Selina Coquire	1000	1200		525.60
				Mary Coquire	300	500		219.
				John Coquire	300	500		131.40
				Annette Coquire	150	200	3100	87.60	1611.30
" "	462	James M. Wright	2	William Brown	2000	1300		569.40
		and Mary A. Wright		Maria Brown	1400	1000	2300	438.
" "	463	Jane N. C. Scott	5	William Johnson		1250		547.50
				Charles Johnson		1300		569.40
				Susan Johnson	5300	100		43.80
				Mary Clare Johnson		1150		503.70
				Mary Johnson		350	4150	153.30
" "	464	Susanna P. Bryan	2	Stephen Hagan	500	550		240.90
				Caroline Henson	300	300	50	131.40
" "	465	Thompson Nailor	3	Albert Dickman	500	500		197.10
				Ann Adams	1000	1000		438.
				Maria Johnson	200	200		87.60

Owner's list from committee work (from District of Columbia Office of the Secretary)

Report of the Commissioners

38th Congress, 1st Session Doc. 42
February 17, 1864

As per the DC Emancipation Act, a commission was set up for its implementation. The commission, as selected by Abraham Lincoln, consisted of Daniel Goodloe, Horatio King, and Samuel Vinton.

The commissioners did not allow the loss of the services of Mr. Vinton deter them, but replaced him with John Brodhead, and delivered their final report on February 17, 1864. The report included a full list of those slaveholders who requested compensation for their slaves, as well as the names of all the slaves for whom such compensation was requested.

The report also includes the results of the implementation of the supplemental act.

38th Congress } HOUSE OF REPRESENTATIVES. { Ex. Doc
1st Session. }   { No. 42

EMANCIPATION IN THE DISTRICT OF COLUMBIA.

LETTER

FROM

THE SECRETARY OF THE TREASURY,

IN ANSWER TO

A resolution of the House of Representatives, of the 11th of January, transmitting the report and tabular statements of the commissioners appointed in relation to emancipated slaves in the District of Columbia.

February 17, 1864.—Laid on the table and ordered to be printed.

Treasury Department, February 16, 1864.

Sir: In accordance with the resolution of the House of Representatives adopted on the 11th ultimo, I have the honor to transmit herewith the report and tabular statements made to me by the commissioners appointed by the President in accordance with the provisions of an act entitled "An act for the release of certain persons held to service or labor in the District of Columbia," approved April 16, 1862, and an act supplementary thereto, approved July 12, 1862.

With great respect,

S. P. CHASE,

Secretary of the Treasury.

Hon. Schuyler Colfax.

Speaker of the House of Representatives, Washington.

OFFICE OF THE COMMISSIONERS UNDER THE ACT OF APRIL 16, 1862, ENTITLED "AN ACT FOR THE RELEASE OF CERTAIN PERSONS HELD TO SERVICE OR LABOR IN THE DISTRICT OF COLUMBIA"

City Hall, *Washington City, D. C, January* 14, 1863.

The commissioners appointed in pursuance "An Act for the release of certain persons held to service or labor in the District of Columbia" approved April 16, 1862, hereby, in conformity with its provisions, present their

REPORT

The commission, as originally constituted, met at the City Hall on the 28th day of April, by direction of the President, and proceeded to organize by the election of William R. Woodward, esq., for the office of clerk. The marshal of the District of Columbia was sent for, and promptly appointed a deputy to attend upon the commission, and to execute its processes. A messenger was appointed from the necessity of the case, though not specially provided for by the act, at a salary of sixty dollars per month. Public notice was given through the newspapers of the city of Washington that the commission would meet daily, except Saturdays, in the City Hall, for the reception and examination of petitions for compensation, in which specific directions for drawing the same were given, as well as of the schedule required by the act, to be filed with the clerk of the circuit court. To facilitate the investigation under the act, and as a matter of public convenience, a blank form for the petitions was prepared by the commissioners, which was printed and sold by a publisher.

Daniel Reaves Goodloe (1814–1902) was an abolitionist from North Carolina. He was a journalist and lawyer. He had been working for the *National Era* when Lincoln was elected, and thereafter became the Washington Correspondent of the *New York Times*.

Samuel Finley Vinton (1792–1862) was born in Massachusetts, and represented Ohio in the House of Representatives from 1823 to 1837, and 1843 to 1851.

In these preliminary arrangements for entering upon their labors the commissioners had the benefit of the legal learning and experience of the Hon. Samuel F. Vinton; but hardly were they completed when the relentless hand of death, by a sudden stroke, severed a connexion which promised to be as useful to the public as it was agreeable to his colleagues. He died on Sunday, the eleventh day of May, after a brief illness. The vacancy thus created in the board was filled by the appointment of John M. Brodhead, who entered upon the discharge of his duties on the fourteenth day of June.

By the terms of the act the claimants for compensation were required to file their petitions within three months from the date of its approval. This period expired on the fifteenth day of July. The whole number of petitions presented during this time was nine hundred and sixty-six, and the number of "persons held to service or labor" embraced in the petitions, for whom compensation was claimed, is three thousand one hundred. In order to secure the government against imposition, a complete list of the names of the petitioners, together with those of the servants claimed by them, was made out by order of the commissioners, and published in all the newspapers of the city, as a means of eliciting evidence to rebut claims founded in fraud, or emanating from persons whom the law designed to exclude on the ground of disloyalty.

After a careful investigation they have reported favorably upon nine hundred and nine (909) entire petitions; they have rejected, entirely, thirty-six petitions, and in part, twenty-one petitions, for the reasons which will be found stated in their order. The whole number of servants for which compensation has been awarded is two thousand nine hundred and eighty-nine, and the whole number of servants for whom compensation has been withheld is one hundred and eleven, making a total of three thousand one hundred, included in the nine hundred and sixty-six petitions.

At the threshold of their labors the commissioners were impressed with the importance of having full information as to the value of slaves, independently of that to be derived from the claimants and their witnesses. The law fixes the maximum average of value, within which limitation the commissioners are required to "appraise and apportion" the value in money of the several claims.

There are few persons, especially in a community like Washington, where slavery has been for many years an interest of comparatively trifling importance, who possess the knowledge and discrimination as to the value of slaves which are necessary

John Montgomery Brodhead was born in New Hampshire, became a doctor, and was later Second Comptroller of the treasury, a post he held until 1857, and again from 1863 to 1876. While a commissioner, he was also a DC Alderman.

Horatio King (1811–1897) was a journalist and later postmaster general for a few months in 1861, having worked his way up from a clerk in the post office. After retiring, he became a lawyer as well as working to complete the Washington Monument.

B. M. Campbell, along with his brother William, was a slave dealer in Baltimore. They had been in business since at least 1835, taking over Hope Slatter's slave jail on Pratt Street in 1852. A half year after the commissioners filed their report, on July 24,Campbell's jail was closed by Colonel William Birney, who showed up, recruited the men into the 4th United States Colored Troops regiment of the Union Army, and freed the women. General emancipation in Maryland did not occur until November 1, 1864.

to a just apportionment of compensation under the law.

None of the commissioners could lay claim to this species of information, and to supply it they determined to summon to their aid an experienced dealer in slaves from Baltimore, Mr. B. M. Campbell, who was at the same time ignorant, in almost every instance, of the individuals upon whose claims he was called to pass judgment. His testimony accorded with that of others whose information in the premises was entitled to weight, that in the disturbed state of the country, since the commencement of the war, it would be difficult to assign value to slaves. The sales have been few, and generally under circumstances of pecuniary pressure which left no discretion with the seller. Slaves, in fact, cannot be said to have had a current salable value since the commencement of the war, while their intrinsic value on tho sixteenth day of April, as determined by the undiminished value of the products of the soil, and the, undiminished wages of labor, was not less than formerly. Indeed, in both these respects it was greater, since there has been a constant rise of prices, both of labor and of products. The minutes of evidence taken by the commissioners furnish sufficient data to establish an actual value of slaves, in many eases far greater than the allowance of compensation made by the law.

Many families derive their chief, if not their sole, support from the hire of their servants, while the others were saved a large annual expense by employing their servants at home. Yet, to make an actual appraisement of three thousand slaves, upon data such as these facts furnish, and in the absence of a current salable value, would hare been an almost interminable labor, and the commissioners felt that they could not fulfil [sic] the duty assigned to them within the time limited by law, by adopting that mode of valuation. Every appraisement, whether of real or personal property, has reference, as well to current sales as to intrinsic value, the current sales furnishing a convenient standard by which to apportion the value of each object. But in the case before them the commissioners had no such standard; and therefore, as a means of arriving at a fair classification of the slaves, according to their intrinsic utility to their owners, and with a view to the completion of their labors within the time limited by law, they adopted the plan of first classifying the slaves according to their value before the commencement of the war, when sales were frequent, and then reducing these classifications to the average compensation allowed by law.

To prevent all misunderstanding, it is stated distinctly that the values assigned by the expert, Mr. Campbell, were by him referred back to the years 1859–1860. It was not pretended by him that slaves on the 16th day of April last were worth the prices named by him. On the contrary, when interrogated upon oath, he declared that there had been no sales, and that no salable value existed since the early part of 1861. His books, exhibited to the commissioners, show that from February 2 to May 18, 1861, his purchases amounted to thirty-seven slaves, at an average cost of six hundred and thirty-six dollars and seventy-five cents. Of these, four are described as children, but perhaps the greater portion of them were in the prime of life. Since May, 1861, he had ceased to purchase, as all communication with the south was then cut off.

Other witnesses, who from time to time were called upon for their opinions, concurred entirely with Mr. Campbell as to the former and present value of slaves.

The classification thus made was necessary to a fair apportionment of compensation among the claimants, and the commissioners are happy to state that nearly universal satisfaction has been given in this particular. But it must be apparent that the actual amount awarded is not dependent upon this classification. The law has given the commissioners the discretion of fixing the average compensation at any sum not exceeding three hundred dollars. It became their duty to determine what average should be allowed; and upon the grounds stated above, that is to say, the enhanced rather than diminished prices of labor and products, they decided the maximum named in the law. The classification would have answered equally well for any lower rate of compensation.

The table marked A, herewith presented, embraces a complete list of the petitions filed within the time limited by law, with the names of the claimants and their slaves, together with the compensation allowed for each slave, and the aggregate to each claimant. In the table will be found, also, the claims which have been in whole or in part rejected, for the reasons set opposite to them respectively, together with the names of the contestants, where conflicting claims have been presented.

An extract of the handwritten original of Table A can be seen on p. 72. The report also contained all the individual cases, printed.

There are four or five cases in which the petitioners have assigned their claims in part, the amount so assigned being awarded accordingly. In a few instances the slaves were hold for a term of years, or for the life of the owner. In such cases the allowances for compensation have been made in proportion to the length of the time and the value of the servant. In like manner, where agreements had been entered into with servants to emancipate them on the payment of a stipulated sum, the amount actually paid has been deducted from the compensation awarded. In several instances claimants held slaves as security for the payment of a specific sum of money. In such cases, if the holder of the reversionary title also claims, the compensation has been apportioned between them. If the latter omitted to claim, the specific claimant alone has been compensated to the extent of his debt. Where slaves have been left by will or otherwise to a person for life, with remainder to children, the award has been made to the owner of the life estate, leaving it to the orphans' court to secure the interests of the chidren. [sic]

A number of paragraphs dealing with individual cases has been excised at this point.

...

There are a few other cases in which the claimants have failed to appear or to produce the slaves for whom compensation in claimed. They are indicated under the head of "remarks" in the table.

As it regards the question of loyalty, there are [b]ut few instances in which the evidence was of a nature to warrant the commissioners in withholding compensation. There are several cases in which there is strong evidence that the petitioners entertained sympathies inconsistent with the idea of a true loyalty. But in the absence of proof that they have borne arms against "the government of the United States in the present rebellion, or in any way given aid or comfort thereto," the commissioners have not felt warranted in withholding compensation, where the law has in other respects been complied with.

The words here cited from the act are contained in the proviso in the third section, the object of which is to declare who shall not receive compensation. They must, therefore, be regarded as intended to explain and define the merely descriptive words contained in the second section. These latter words are as follows: "That all persons *loyal* to the United States holding claims to service or labor against persons discharged therefrom by this act may," &c.

The words of the proviso to the third section are almost identical with those of the Constitution which define treason. The third section of the third article declares that "treason against the United States shall consist only in levying war against them, or in adhering to their enemies, giving them aid and comfort. No person shall be convicted of treason unless on the testimony of two witnesses to the same overt act or on confession in open court."

It is also true that the "forfeiture" provided for in the Constitution as one of the punishments of treason, is similar in its effects to the exclusion from compensation provided for by the act of emancipation.

Under such circumstances the commissioners have felt bound

to be governed by the general principles of construction applied by the courts of this country to the third section of the third article of the Constitution, and by the English courts to the statute of treason.

It is to be remarked, also, that this rule for the interpretation of the emancipation act is entirely consistent with the Constitution itself, while a different one, which should entirely confiscate the property of a citizen as a punishment for his unpatriotic sentiments, would be inconsistent with it.

The three cases of this kind, in which the evidence of unpatriotic or disloyal sympathies is most manifest, are those of ladies advanced in years. They were required, like all other petitioners, to take the oath of allegiance and to produce two witnesses to attest their loyalty. The law being thus complied with, and in the absence of any evidence that they had given "aid and comfort" to the rebellion, the commissioners have had no alternative but to make them proportionate allowance of compensation.

By the terms of the act of emancipation, every slave held to service in the. District of Columbia was set free on the 16th day of April, and ceased to be under the control of his former master.

Most of them immediately left their homes and sought employment from others: many of them left the District of Columbia to join the service of officers of the army, or to go north. Under such circumstances it would be manifestly unjust to withhold compensation on account of the inability of the claimant to produce the servant before the commissioners.

They have, therefore, first required an oath from the claimant as to bis inability to produce his servants, and that he had used due diligence in his efforts to find them, and then received the testimony if competent witnesses as to the age, size, complexion, health and qualifications of such absent servants, and have appraised them upon the description thus furnished, always, however, as a security against imposition, and as an incitement to the claimants to use due diligence, abating something from the appraisement which would be just, if the servants were present and corresponded with the description. The same rule has been applied to the case of slaves who have died since the passage of the act.

Several claims have been put in for slaves who absconded prior to the 16th of April, 1862. In these cases both the claimants and the slaves were interested in favor of a construction of the act which would entitle the owner to compensation. In some instances the fugitives came back in order to avail themselves of the benefit of the act. But in others this was not the case. The commissioners, after a careful investigation, have decided, that where the owner of the fugitive could give evidence that he had used ordinary diligence to recover his slave, and where the lapse of time has raised no presumption of death, or abandonment, compensation may be allowed.

It is a well-settled principle of law in the slaveholding States, that a slave cannot acquire a residence without the consent of the owner, actual or implied. The home of a fugitive slave, therefore, is, in contemplation of the laws recognizing slavery, the home of his master, or that in which his master had placed him. The decisions on this point in the courts of the slave States [sic] are numerous, and are parallel to those of the English and American courts as to the domicile of the wife, which is that of the husband, even though her actual residence is different from his. It would seem to follow from this state of things that, in point of law, the fugitives from the District of Columbia whose legal domicile is here, were set free by the emancipation act of April 16, and that the owners have no longer any right to recover them under the law for the return of fugitives from labor. The commissioners will not cumber their report by the citation of authorities on these points, and content themselves with stating the principles on which they have acted.

But if the fugitives were made free by the emancipation act, it would seem to result, as a matter of course, that the owners are entitled to compensation; and on this ground compensation has been awarded in several instances for fugitives under the limitations above stated. The allowance of compensation for fugitive slaves, whose actual residence and existence are not known as a fact, is based on the legal presumption familiar to the courts of this country and of England, that "when the existence of a person, a personal relation, or a state of things, is once established by proof, the law presumes that the person, relation, or state of things continues to exist as before, till the contrary is shown, or till a different presumption is raised from the nature of the subject in question. Thus, where the issue is upon the *life* or death of a person once shown to have been living, the burden of proof lies upon the party who asserts the death. But after the lapse of seven years, without intelligence concerning the person, the presumption of life ceases, and the burden of proof is devolved on the other party. (*Greenleaf's Evidence, vol.* 1, *page* 48.)

Simon Greenleaf, *A Treatise on the Law of Evidence,* Boston: Little, Brown, and Company, 1853.

On this rule of evidence the most sacred rights of men are made to turn every day in the courts of law and the commissioners feel that they have no right to exclude it in the adjudication of claims under the emancipation act. They have, however, allowed no claim where the slave had been absent longer than two years, or where he had not been heard from within a few months.

The effect of a literal construction of the act in this and the other respects referred to above has been to extend its benefits to several slaves and their owners, who, though within its equity, would be excluded by a narrow adherence to the letter. The commissioners are warranted in acting upon this equitable vale by the highest legal authority; but one citation from Chancellor Kent will suffice:

"Statutes," he says, "that are remedial and not penal are to receive an *equitable* interpretation, by which the *letter* the act is sometimes restrained and sometimes *enlarged*, so as more effectually to meet the beneficent end in view and prevent a failure of the object." So say all the authorities.

James Kent. *Commentaries on American Law, Volume 1.* Tenth Ed. Boston: Little, Brown and Company, 1860. Kent (1763–1847) was an American Jurist and the Chancellor of New York. This book (in the 12th Edition, edited by Oliver Wendell Holmes,) remains in print today.

THE SUPPLEMENTARY ACT.

By the second section of the supplementary act, approved July 12, 1862, it was made the duty of the commissioners to investigate and decide the claims to freedom of those persons who had been held to service in the District of Columbia by reason of African descent, for whom compensation had not been claimed by their former owners. To this end such servants were authorized to file a statement or schedule setting forth the facts, with the clerk of the circuit court.

It was also provided by the 4th section of the supplementary act "that all persons held to service or labor under the laws of any State, and who, at any time since the sixteenth day of April, anno Domini eighteen hundred and sixty two, by the consent of the person to whom such service or labor is claimed to be owing, have been actually employed within the District of Columbia, or who shall be hereafter thus employed, are hereby declared free and forever released from such services, anything in the laws of the United States or of any State to the contrary notwithstanding."

The whole number of petitions which have been brought before the commissioners under the supplementary act is one hundred and sixty-one, of which one hundred and thirty-nine have been granted and twenty-two rejected, in the absence of proof, or, more generally, because the evidence made it clear that the petitioner's case was not provided for by the act.

Again, individual cases have been omitted at this point.

...

Table B contains a complete list of petitioners under the supplementary act, with the names of the former owners, and the witnesses called by the parties; also an alphabetical list of persons to whom certificates of freedom have been granted, together with

those from whom certificates have been withheld.
All of which is respectfully submitted.

DANIEL R. GOODLOE,

HORATIO KING

J. M. BRODHEAD,

Commissioners

Hon. Salmon P. Chase
Secretary of the Treasury

LINCOLN WISHED HIS WORK WAS DONE.
Daniel R. Goodloe, in the Washington Star.

I had the honor of being appointed by Mr. Lincoln, in 1862, as one of the three Commissioners under the Emancipation act to pay the people of the District of Columbia for their slaves. It was a work of no little labor and responsibility, and we were nearly nine months in completing it. Our report was returnable to the Secretary of the Treasury, but in the absence of Mr. Chase at the time my colleagues (the Hon. Horatio King. Dr. John M. Brodhead) and myself concluded to call, with our clerk, Mr. Woodward, upon the President, and announce the conclusion of our labors. He received us pleasantly and said he was "glad to know that somebody had finished something," and that he " wished his work was done."

New York Times, December 27, 1887 (from NYTimes.com)

The Emancipation of the Slaves of the District of Columbia

Rev. Page Milburn, Ph.D
Records of the Columbia Historical Society
April 16, 1912

Newspaper accounts of the time are quite silent on the public response to the signing of the DC Emancipation Act. Both the *Intelligencer* and the *Evening Star* were against the act (as, apparently, were most DC residents) and so mainly quoted other sources who were darkly prognosticating violent upheaval because of its passage. It is therefore necessary to jump ahead 50 years in order to see what the reaction amongst the freed slaves as well as other African-Americans was.

The Rev. Page Milburn wrote a paper, presented before the Columbia Historical Society in 1912, in which he gave an overview of the history of emancipation in the District of Columbia, the discussions of the bill—both in Congress and in the local papers—as well as describing the reactions thereto. In this excerpt, Milburn describes the reactions of those most affected by the new law: the freed slaves themselves.

Of the 'day of thanksgiving' mentioned below, no trace shows up in the newspapers of the day. The closest is the *Evening Star,* which published, on May 1, 1862, a short article entitled "Slaves Returning Home," describing two 'contrabands' who left their master in Prince George's County in hopes of finding freedom in the District. Finding that their free compatriots in the District were overwhelmingly unemployed, they had decided to return to their master. The article is written in the usual condescending matter, with their dialect rendered with a surfeit of apostrophes.

Other sources state that the main celebration was held on April 20, and that "every Negro church in the city

"The Emancipation of the Slaves in the District of Columbia" by Rev. Page Milburn, Ph.D., *Records of the Columbia Historical Society, Washington DC. Volume 16.* Columbia Historical Society, Washington DC, 1913.

Benjamin
Quarles,
*Lincoln and
the Negro,*
New York,
Oxford
University
Press, 1962.

held special services of prayer and thanksgiving. The proceedings did not always conform to the established rites for public worship, as church members were singing, shouting, praying, weeping, or jumping, all without direction from the pulpit."

The Rev. Milburn unfortunately does not mention from what source he extracted the resolutions.

That there was great rejoicing among the negroes of the District of course goes without saying. At this day their solemn declarations make interesting reading.

A few days after President Lincoln signed the bill making free many who hitherto had been slaves, the colored people of the District held a convention in the colored Presbyterian Church, and passed the following resolutions:

"1. Resolved, That we return our most devout thanks to Almighty God, who in his great wisdom and mercy has governed and controlled the current events of time, so as to bring to us of this District that dearest of all earthly treasures—Freedom. And that we first offer to Him the true homage of our grateful hearts for this sacred and invaluable blessing.

"2. Resolved, That by our industry, energy, moral deportment and character, we will prove ourselves worthy of the confidence reposed in us in making us free men.

"3. Resolved, That to the citizens of the District of Columbia we give our sincere assurance that as in the past we have as a people been orderly and law abiding, so in the future we shall strive with might and main, to be in every way worthy of the glorious privileges which have now been conferred upon us.

"4. Resolved, ' ... a resolution of heartfelt and enduring thanks to Congress, to President Lincoln and to our friends generally.'

"5. A resolution fixing Thursday May 1, 1862, as a day of thanksgiving and directing that these resolutions be read in every colored congregation, Sunday, April 27, 1862."

The Emancipation Jubilee Last Night

Washington Evening Star
April 17, 1863

A year after DC emancipation, the newspapers (or at least the *Evening Star*) had resigned themselves to the question, and deigned to cover the anniversary celebration. The reporter, other than taking great umbrage at the idea that slavery can be compared to "a dragon," exhibiting a certain level of condescension, and running out of steam before all the speakers have finished, gives a fairly even-handed account of the evening in the following article.

All brackets are as in the original, unless indicated.

The Emancipation Jubilee Last Night

The anniversary of the signing of the act for the emancipation of the slaves of the District of Columbia was celebrated last evening by a demonstration in the 15th street Presbyterian Church, (colored.)

This church is well known as the aristocratic colored church of the District, with cushioned seats, carpeted aisles, gold-lettered pews, marble-topped pulpit stand, handsome chandeliers, a fair organ, and a choir of no little celebrity. Caucasians hurrying away from the damnable discords of their own church choirs, sometimes pause at the doors of the Fifteenth street church to hear the rich swell and fine harmonies if Grant's choir, or the delicate grace of Boston's voluntaries. It is a well-dressed congregation Nowhere have we seen finer bonnets than here last night. Altogether, the gathering and style of celebration was very different from that at the contraband camp New Years night, addressed by rude speakers of the "John de Baptis" stripe. With a

The 15th Street Presbyterian Church was founded in 1841 by John F. Cook, Sr. His son, John F. Cook Jr., took over the ministry in 1855. The church was located on 15th Street, between I and K Streets.

single exception, last night, where a colored speaker used the scarcely defensible figure of representing slavery as "a dragon scattering lava throughout the land," the speaking, both in matter and manner, was quite as good, if not better, than that which usually prevails at "demonstrations" amongst white folks.

On the platform were seated John F. Cook, who presided, T. H. C. Hinton, of New York, artist, Rev. Mr. Shelton, of Cincinnati, J. E. Green, of Detroit, Mich., J. Willis Menard, poet, W. E. Matthews, of Baltimore, Rev. Mr. Turner, (white) late chaplain of the 4th Pa. Cavalry, who is here on business relating to recruiting colored soldiers. Among the audience we noticed Rev. S. P. Hill, Dr. Breed, J. D. Harris, (colored.) of the Haytien Bureau of emigration, in uniform.

Major Alexander T. Augusta was the first (of eight) African-Americans who were commissioned as physicians during the Civil War. He later had a highly regarded practice in DC.

The appearance of a colored man in the room wearing the gold leaf epaulettes of a Major, was also the occasion of much applause and gratulation with the assembly. The individual thus distinguished was Dr. A. T Augusta, who received an assistant Surgeon's commission last week from the Secretary of War. He is a native of Virginia, and graduated at Trinity College, Toronto, Canada.

The demonstration was under the management of Mrs. Kechbey, president of the Ladies Contraband Relief Association, S. J. Datcher, William Slade and others of note amongst the colored people of the district.

About 8 o'clock the meeting was called to order by John F. Cook, (son of the well-known colored preacher,) who introduced Rev. Mr. Shelton, (colored,) of Cincinnati, who offered up a prayer in which blessings were invoked on the members of Congress who passed the decree abolishing slavery, and the President for the measures he had taken to liberate the slaves of the country.

Thomas Hinton was a African Methodist Episcopal minister.

Mr. Thos. H. C. Hinton, (col.,) of New York, was the first speaker. On the 16th of April 1862, a law was promulgated making liberty paramount to slavery at the seat of the national jurisprudence of the country. President Lincoln made the law secure by his approval, [applause;] and that people which had heretofore been kept under the iron heel of oppression stood forth clothed in liberty. In this act the right conquered might. [Applause.] Slavery, which had been maintained by a legion of political devils, regardless of the tears and entreaties of mother, wife, or children, was partially done away with. The people now left the dark picture of the past and beheld a gleam of liberty. The country was no longer under an incubus, and with a massive blow the hydra-headed monster was felled to death. Notice this dear baby of the country, this political pet of the South, this cherubim of the F. F. V's, and we cannot do better than to look at it as it has developed itself.

Let any one even to-day have but a drop of African blood in their veins, and let him or her pass or approach one of the slaveocrats, and the first word you hear from them is, "Hello nigger!" Any man or woman, if of African descent, is thus subject continually to a vile vituperation. There is no redress when thus assaulted, unless you redress yourselves and take the law into your own hands. And the law is simply for the white man and not for the black, Again, if an African seeks accommodation in a street railroad car, he is told by the conductor, "We don't accommodate niggers in this car," and this is one of the features of slavery as it exists in our midst. If this is the case to-day, what was it before the issue of the Emancipation Proclamation. Must we not then do all to conquer this great prejudice and to destroy this fiery dragon that is scattering its devastating lava about our land. The colored man loved liberty. It was a gift of the great and good God, and it was intended as the path in which all should walk. If it shall appear in the course of human events that there was a prospect of a higher development of the colored race, they must endeavor to meet the event by making themselves better. Whose hand was it that had struck the deathblow to slavery but that of Abraham Lincoln. [Applause.] They (the colored people) rejoiced with a loud voice and hailed with joy his advent among them. [Applause.] May his path be strewn with peace and prosperity, [applause,] and may the nation look upon him as the repairer of the land and the restorer of the National paths. [Applause.]

J. Willis Menard (colored poet) was next introduced. One year ago to-day, he said, the sun of slavery sunk down into its native hell, [applause,] and buried in the fall the clash of devilish chains, [renewed applause,] and the Capital of the Nation ceased to be the great workshop of fetters and chains for the negro. The colored people leaped from the condition of brutes to the broad and lasting platform of humanity. [Applause.] By emancipation thousands have been thrown upon them (the colored people), and they must choose for them. They must plan for them and teach them the great lessons of man and woman and husband and wife. They (the colored people) have a work of humanity to perform, and action! Action! Action! is called for. [Applause.] The negro race are a part of the people of this great country, but have always been looked upon in degradation. The most lucrative avocations were almost wholly reserved as a dignified reward to those of a lighter complexion. Yet with all this—with hands bound, and with the heel of tyranny upon them, the colored race have been

The acronym F.F.V refers to "First Families of Virginia."

John Willis Menard (1838–1893) was a journalist and civil rights leader as well as a poet. In 1862, he was a clerk in the Interior Department, charged with finding possible locations for colonies of freed slaves. He is said to be the first African-American to hold a white-collar job in government.

taunted with inferiority, and told to show their statesmen, their learned men, and their jurists. We see the poor, miserable African, way back in the dim twilight of remembrance and when the grass was yet wet with the dews of creation's morn, that race were unrivaled in literature, art and science [Applause.] We see with pain the loss of these arts now, but notwithstanding this, the Africans have been the teachers of the world in civilization and the arts. [Applause.] He proceeded to compare the Egyptians (claimed by him as their ancestors) to the Britons, to at all to the advantage of the latter. When carried to Greece and Rome as slaves, the Britons proved too stupid to make even good servants [laughter] and from that boasted race descended Abraham Lincoln. [Great laughter.]

The claims of suffering humanity will find a response in every human heart; and a spirit of benevolence was now being diffused over our bloodstained land. He (the speaker) believed Abraham Lincoln was commissioned from Heaven the great engineer to carry out the great work. [Applause.] Of all the Presidents and notwithstanding the glories that cluster around the name of Washington, the name of Abraham Lincoln would be heard in thunder in ages yet to come. [Loud applause.] The contrabands were in the midst of the colored race. But they shall not be called contrabands. Thy were men and brethren. They were not free, nor are we the free colored. The colored race must carve out its own destiny. They are men and must venture as do the whites. [Cries of "That's so."] Many of the negroes have prejudices against emigration. The speaker then referred to the divisions upon the question of abolition and colonization. The first had given them Fred. Douglass, [applause,] McCune Smith and the other little stars that revolve around him. The other had given them two great nationalities. [Applause.] When men become educated the darkness of slavery must retreat. For 350 years there had been no quietude between the races. The Americans were jealous of their liberty, and man, whenever he is in the ascendency, [sic -ed.] is disposed to to be semi-despotic.

The speaker then congratulated the audience on the fact that, for the first time in the history of this country, epaulettes were seen upon the shoulders of a black man. [Tremendous applause.] (The presence of Dr. Augusta in full surgeon's uniform called out this remark.) Could he only see a major general's epaulettes on a black man, he would cease to be an emigrationist. [Laughter and applause.]

The speaker concluded by reciting the following poem, which he had prepared for the occasion:

Dr. James McCune Smith (1813–1865) was the first African-American medical doctor, having received his degree from the University of Glasgow (Scotland) He was also an abolitionist, working with Frederick Douglass.

ONE YEAR AGO TO-DAY

Dedicated to the Emancipated Slaves of the District of Columbia.

Almighty God! We praise thy name,
For having head us pray
For having freed us from our chains,
One year ago to-day.

We thank thee, for thy arm has stayed
Foul despotism's sway
And made Columbia's District free,
One year ago to-day.

Give us the power to withstand
Oppression's baneful fray;
That right may triumph as it did,
One year ago to-day.

Give liberty to millions yet
'Neath despotism's sway,
That they may praise thee as *we* did,
One year ago to-day.

O! guide us safely through this storm;
Bless Lincoln's gentle sway,
And then we'll ever praise thee, as
One year ago to-day.

Only one volume of Menard's poetry has ever been published: *Lays in Summer Lands* was published by Enterprise Publishing in 1879. This poem was not included.

[The recital of this poem elicited great applause.]

The next speaker introduced was J. F. Green, (colored,) of Michigan, who said that the the American Revolution was an important epoch in the world history; not only having its effect on the whites, but upon the blacks. He alluded to the blacks helping to fight for our liberties, and instanced W. C. Will, a black of Boston, who shed the first blood. Crispus Attux [sic -ed.] another black man, fell at the head of a band of citizens in the Boston massacre. Colored blood was spilt at Bunker Hill, and the bones of the blacks repose there with the whites. In Rhode Island a regiment of blacks was raised, and in Connecticut a large battalion who fought bravely throughout the war, but owing to the prejudices of the whites their deeds have been covered up.

He alluded to a speech made by Charles Pinckney, of South Carolina, in which he admitted that during the war of the revolution colored men fought bravely with the whites. The victory at New Orleans was won by blacks as well as whites, who

Charles Pinckney (1757–1824) was a signer of the Constitution, governor of South Carolina, Senator and Congressman.

On February 14, 1820 Pinckney gave a stirring defence of slave representation from the South: "And it is a remarkable fact that, notwithstanding, in the course of the Revolution, Southern States were continually overrun by the British, and every negro in them had an opportunity of running away, yet few did. They then were, as they still are, as valuable a part of our population to the Union as any other equal number of inhabitants."
He was the father of Henry Pinckney. (see p. 13)

Owen Lovejoy (1811–1864) represented Illinois in the House of Representatives from 1857 to 1864. He was a lawyer, minister, and abolitionist.
For more on Senator Wilson, see p. 53.

were highly complimented by General Jackson. He contended that patriotism was more deeply rooted in the blacks than in the whites. They pour out their blood for those who do not regard them as fellow man.

He then referred to the progress made in liberating slaves in different portions of the earth. The English slaves liberated by their Irish masters did not rebel against their deliverers. In Chili every child born after the 10th of October, 1811, was declared free. In Columbia every slave bearing arms was emancipated July 19, 1821, and provisions were made for the emancipation of the remainder, amounting to 280,000. In Mexico, September 15, 1829, instant and unconditional freedom was given every slave. At the Cape of Good Hope, 30,000 Hottentots were freed in 1823. In all these places without unhappy results. The slaves in the British dominions West Indies, amounting to 830,000, were liberated; and in 1848 slavery through the British dominions was abolished, by which 12,000,000 in the Eat Indies were liberated.

On the 1st of January, 1863, the President's proclamation declared free 435,132 in Alabama, 111,104 in Arkansas, 61,753 in Florida, 462,232 in Georgia, 436696 in Mississippi, 402,411 in South Carolina, 480,682 in Texas, which amounts to 2,098,440; and in Louisiana excepting New Orleans 318,531; in North Carolina, excepting Beaufort, 331,081; Tennessee, excepting loyal portions, 275,785; Virginia, excepting West Virginia, 440,897; making a total of 3,456,121 who were declared free by the proclamation.

Russia has emancipated 7,000,000 slaves, and in our country, with 3,000,000 square miles, heretofore there was not a place in which a fugitive could be safe.

William E. Mathews, (colored,) was then introduced. He said it was a custom as old as antiquity for men to come together to celebrate great events. The Jews celebrated the Passover; England the birthday of her Queen. All the great powers of the earth, including Hayti and Liberia, (applause,) have a day peculiarly their own. The white Americans celebrate the Fourth of July. But it is an unhappy fact that the colored people of the United States had no day to celebrate. Thank God, another and a better day has at last dawned, (applause,) and this evening the colored people met under circumstances never before known. Wilson and Lovejoy (applause,) would be handed down to posterity with blessings. [Applause.]

The speaker hoped that the 16th day of April would ever be a day of rejoicing in this District. [Applause.] Let the rejoicing swell the ride until all in the United States meet in one grand celebration; [applause,] and when the colored men shall stand on one grand platform of universal right. [Applause.] He liked these anniversaries. They inspired them with a manhood they did not feel on other occasions. [Applause.]

The colored people should celebrate the birthdays of their great men—the birthday of Hannibal, who crossed the Alps and compelled the Romans to cringe at his feet, [applause,] of Toussaint l'Ouverture, [applause,] who worked successfully the greater than mathematical problem that they who would be free must first strike the blow. [Applause,] He (l'Ouverture) had turned Hayti from a hell of slavery to a paradise of freedom, (applause;) and America had been forced to recognize her nationality, and to-day we have a black man [applause] representing her here. He would like also to see celebrated the birthday of Benj. Banneker, the negro astronomer, who first gave an Almanac to Maryland, Virginia and the District. [Applause.] Who were the early fathers of religion? Who put the light to the torch of christianity, which has continued to burn brightly, but St. Cyprian, Augustine and others of their race? He would like to see their memories celebrated. [Applause.] He could name a great many more, both of ancient and modern days, but so long as history does its duty the names of these men will never be forgotten. Let us, then, believe that this is te beginning of a better time for the race. In conclusion, this speaker also recited a poem of his own composition appropriate to the occasion.

Other speakers followed, Francis Taverns (colored), Dr. Breed, Judge Day, and others, but for whose remarks we have not space to-day.

The affair concluded with some musical exercises in the basement of the church. "Vive la America" and several pieces, including the "John Brown's Song," were sung during the evening by Misses Margaret Brown, M. Cookley, L. Starr, and F. Fisher, and Messrs. T. S. Boston and W. F. Landie, with much effect.

Benjamin Banneker was a free African-American surveyor mathematician and almanac author. He was hired by Major Ellicott to survey the land that was to become the District of Columbia. From 1792 until 1797, Banneker published an almanac including weather forecasts, tide tables, eclipses and other such information.

John W. Menard addresses the House of Representatives on February 27, 1869. From *Frank Leslie's Illustrated Newspaper,* March 20, 1869. (from Library of Congress)

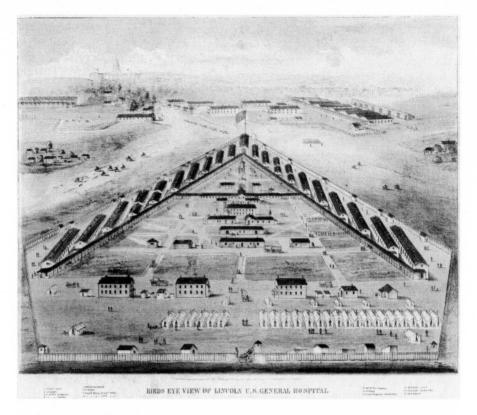

Birds Eye View of Lincoln U.S. General Hospital. Lithograph with copyright registered to Charles H. Seymour, printed by Sanders & Co., Baltimore ca. 1865. (from Library of Congress)

Lincoln United States Army General Hospital was built in 1861 on a rubble strewn field one mile east of the Capitol. The area on which it was built had been originally destined by Pierre L'Enfant to house a mile marker, from which all distances to and from Washington would be measured. Although the land was taken over by the federal government, nothing was done with the land (nor was much built nearby) and so the reservation became a dumping ground. Originally, the hospital was named ironically after the president, but soon thereafter, it was given this name officially.

The hospital was built of canvas-covered logs, and was considered a model hospital—and a vast improvement over the temporary hospitals built previously around the city in churches and other public buildings.

Lincoln Hospital had 2,575 beds, and was thereby the largest hospital in Washington. (see John Wells Bulkley, "The War Hospitals," in *Washington During War Time,* ed. Marcus Benjamin, Washington, 1902.)

Walt Whitman, who was a frequent visitor, described Lincoln Hospital in an article printed in the *New York Times* of December 11, 1864, "[Carver Hospital] has more inmates than an ordinary country town. The same with Lincoln Hospital, east of the Capitol. ... A wanderer like me about Washington, pauses on some high land which commands the sweep of the city...and has his eyes attracted by these white clusters of barracks in almost every direction."

Although Lincoln often visited the hospitals around the city, there is no evidence indicating that he visited this hospital. However, a doctor assigned to Lincoln hospital was one of the first to offer aid to the President after the attack by John Wilkes Booth.

After the Civil War, the hospital was torn down, but its name was passed on to the ground on which it had been built, first as Lincoln Square, later as Lincoln Park. (See p. 113)

Assistant Quartermaster at the Washington Depot to the Chief Quartermaster of the Depot

Letter
July 31, 1863

The question as to what the freed slaves in DC—both those freed in there and those who either fled the South or were freed by Union soldiers—were to do was immediately apparent. Though some joined the Union army, others looked for work in the District of Columbia.

Freed slaves from the South were universally known as 'Contrabands' and in this letter, the work they do for the hospitals in the District of Columbia is described. The request for the information transmitted in this letter came because it was hoped that they might be reassigned to war duties, while convalescing soldiers could take over the work done by the contrabands.

In the end, it was decided that the soldiers would refuse to do such menial work, and the *status* was left *quo*.

All oddities of spelling and punctuation are from the original.

Washington, D.C., July 31" 1863

General: I have the honor to report, that in accordance with your instructions of the 28" inst. I have examined in to the manner in which the contrabands, reported by Lt. N. W. Carroll, are employed, and respectfully submit the following as the result of such investigation.

At Columbian Hospital there are Eleven (11) men. employed, as follows.(6). Six. Policeing ditching and draining (2) Carrying water & Cleaning floors (2) Two Sawing wood for Hospital Kitchens (1) Surgeon's Waiter & Ostler

Columbian Hospital was on 14th St. in Mt. Pleasant. Carver Hospital was on the grounds of Columbian University (Now George Washington University)

93

Harewood Hospital stood on Corcoran's farm which was on 7th St., near the Soldier's home

Finley Hospital was located near Kendall Green, on Bladensburg Rd, north of Boundary St. (Now Florida ave.)

Emory Hospital stood one mile east of the Capitol, near the alms house and Congressional Cemetery.

Campbell Hospital was Boundary St. between 5th and 6th Sts NW

Camp Hayti is not referenced anywhere else; it was the unofficial name of a contraband camp somewhere in DC.

At Carver Hospital Twenty nine men are employed, as follows. (22) Twenty two. Policeing. Ditching and Draining (2) Two. Sawing wood for Wash House & Laundry. (1) One. Washing Sinks (4) Four, Hauling water for Officers Mess, Stewards Mess & Cooking purposes, removing Slops from wards, Cook House, &c,

At Harewood Hospital Forty nine (40) men are employed as follows. (2) Asst. Cooks. One for Contrabands and One for Clerks Mess, (3) Assistants to Hospital Bakers, (2) Taking Care of Ambulance Horses, (36) Policeing and improving grounds, (1) Grinding Coffee &c. at Hospt. Commissary (3) Sawing wood. Carrying water and hanging out Clothes at Laundry (2) Sawing wood for Wards and Bake House.

At Finley Hospital Thirty Seven (37) men are employed, as follows– (1) One, Assisting Mason (1) One Assisting Carpenter (1) One Assisting Gardner (8) Eight, Cleaning Spittoons, Sinks & Wards. (1) One Ostler for Surgeon's and Ambulance Horses. (2) Two, Pumping Water for, and making fires in Laundry (20) Twenty, Policeing & improving grounds. (3) Three Sawing wood for Surgeon, Clerks, and Laundry.

At Emory Hospital Thirty eight (38) men are employed as follows (3) Chopping wood and making fires in Hospital and Laundry (1) Waiter at Surgeons Quarters, (1) Ostler (1) Waiter at Commissary building (1) Waiter at Dispensary (31) Policeing and improving grounds,

At Lincoln Hospital Fifty One (51) men are employed, as follows, (3) Pumping Water for Hospital. (5) Cleaning Sinks & Quarters (1) Teamster (2) Cooks (40) Policeing and improving grounds

At Armory Square Hospital Twenty Six 26. men are employed (1) One. As Teamster and (25) Twenty five in Policeing Grounds &c

At Campbell Hospital Twelve (12) men are employed in Policeing and improving the grounds

At Camp Hayti, There are Fifty Six (56) men employed as follows (18) Scavengers (3) Cooks for Contraband messes (36) Laborers, burrying horses, night soil &c.

I am informed by Lt. N. W. Carroll that no definite instructions have been given him in regard to the kinds of work for which these men should be employed in Hospitals. The Contrabands have, in most cases, been detailed by the Military Governor, and the Surgeons have considered themselves as having entire control of the men when so detailed and, as above stated, have used them as waiters, Ostlers, for hanging out clothes &c.

I would respectfully recommend that definite instructions be given to Lt. Carroll, with authority to enable him to carry out such instructions, he having been detailed by the Military Governor to take charge of these Contrabands.

The force at the Hospitals could be reduced at least one third, and in my opinion, might be wholly dispensed with, by having the work they now do, done by convalescents. All the scavenger work at the Hospitals is now done by the Camp Hayti Scavengers. I have the honor to be, General, Very Respectfly Your obd Servt,

Scavengers were men on garbage detail.

E. E. Camp

Contrabands in Camp Brightwood, outside Washington DC, summer of 1861. John Shaw was 2nd Lieutenant in the 2nd Rhode Island Regiment from June 6th, 1861 until July 22nd of the same year. (from Library of Congress)

CELEBRATION OF THE ABOLITION OF SLAVERY IN THE DISTRICT OF COLUMBIA BY THE COLORED PEOPLE, IN WASHINGTON, APRIL 19, 1866.—[SKETCHED BY F. DIELMAN.]

"Celebration of the abolition of slavery in the District of Columbia by the colored people, in Washington, April 19, 1866." Print by F. Dielman. The scene is that on Franklin Square. The stages described in the *National Intelligencer* article reprinted below can be seen in the distance. The location that this scene was is Franklin Square, bounded by 13th, 14th, K and I streets NW, a few blocks northeast of the White House. The artist, Frederick Dielman, was a German who had emigrated to the United States as a young child. He was all of 18 when he sketched the emancipation celebration. He had a successful career as an artist, with numerous murals of his, including one in the Library of Congress, in Washington DC.

This print was first published in the *Harper's Weekly* magazine of May, 12, 1866. (from Library of Congress)

The Emancipation Celebration

Daily National Intelligencer
April 19, 1866

Emancipation celebrations as wished for by William E. Mathews on April 16, 1863, did not begin to flourish until 1866. There seem to have been no festivities on that day in 1864 (or possibly the *Star* and *Intelligencer* were once again ignoring them) and Lincoln's assassination put all such ideas on ice the next year. The first major emancipation celebration in the District of Columbia was held on Thursday, April 19, 1866. This was not only the first anniversary of DC Emancipation Day following the end of hostilities between the Union and Confederacy, but also the first post-ratification of the 13th amendment.

That these celebrations would be on a a much grander scale than the preceding ones can be seen by the fact that the *New York Times* not only covered them, but even had a short item announcing their impending arrival on April 18—and dispatched two reporters to cover the actual event.

Under their Washington News header, a section headed "The Emancipation Celebration" read as follows: "All the Senators have received special invitations to attend the emancipation celebration in the city next Thursday [April 19th]. The members of the House have been invited by advertisement. Colored persons in various portions of the country will be represented by delegations."

The full events of the day were covered by all major newspapers, including the *Times.* As an example, the article from the *Daily National Intelligencer* is reprinted below.

Exactly two months later, the first Juneteenth celebrations, which commemorated the first anniversary of the reading of General Granger's "General Order No. 3" in Galveston, TX, was held. General Order No. 3

reiterated the Emancipation Proclamation, and was the
first official announcement thereof to the slaves in
Texas.
Brackets are, unless indicated, from the original.

The Emancipation Celebration
Great Outpouring of Colored People
The Procession, Incidents, etc.
Speech of President Johnson
Mass Meeting in Franklin Square
The Speeches on the Occasion

The colored people of the District of Columbia had made
extensive preparations for the celebration on Monday last of the
fourth annual return of the anniversary of the passage of the act
abolishing slavery in the District of Columbia; but owing to the
bad weather on that day the celebration was postponed until
yesterday, when, as was announced by advertisement, the
demonstration was to take place, "rain or shine," and the day
being a bright and pleasant one, it *did* take place, and was a
perfect success.

At an early hour persons who proposed to participate in the
celebration commenced to assemble at Franklin Square, all of
them being attired in their holiday costume and with well-
polished boots, which, however, after a march through the muddy
streets, hardly looked as though they had been cleaned in the
morning. But the streets were not so bad as might have been
expected by reason of the recent rains, a fine breeze yesterday
morning drying up the mud to a great extent. About nine o'clock
the marshals, mounted upon spirited horses, began to arrive, and
meanwhile enterprising colored people with propensities for
speculation largely developed, had erected booths and stands,
whence they retailed pies, cakes, lemonade, apples, oranges, and,
in some instances, more substantial food. Several houses in the
vicinity were decorated with the national colors.

THE SPEAKER'S STAND

The stand from which the speeches were expected to be delivered
had been erected in the south quarter of the square, about midway
between Thirteenth and Fourteenth streets, and was calculated to
seat at least one hundred persons. It was covered with canvas, and
handsomely decorated—large American flags being suspended at

each side, and festooned all about it while a profusion of smaller flags added beauty and effect to the scene. Seats, which had been placed in front of the stand, were occupied at an early hour by colored women, who had evidently come early to get a good seat, and seemed determined to sit it out, in spite of the rays of the sun, which commenced to beat down very uncomfortably about ten o'clock. On the front of the sand the following inscriptions and mottoes were displayed:

Fellow citizens of the Senate and House of Representatives: The act entitled "An Act for the release of certain persons held to service in the District of Columbia," has this day been approved and signed.

April 16, 1862

A LINCOLN.

"Lincoln, the liberator of millions. His great work is done, and he sleeps in peace in the great prairies of the West." "We are loyal to God and to our country." "This is the Lord's doing, and it is marvelous to our eyes." "We have received our civil rights— Give us the right of suffrage and the work is done."

West of the speaker's stand was a smaller one, which was intended to be occupied by the band.

ASSEMBLING AT THE GROUND

By ten o'clock several hundred persons, among whom were a large number of whites, had assembled in and about the square and the crowd became quite animated, especially when a band was heard in the distance, and gleaming muskets carried by black braves were seen moving down K street. Nearly every one on the south side of the square made a rush to the north side, marshals spurred up their steeds and hurried hither and thither to receive the arriving delegations, and assign each its position. Bands were playing, drums beating, men hurrahing in all directions, while the crowd, which no numbered several thousand, moved to and fro, jostling and pushing each other on the pavement and in the mud, and almost completely filling Franklin square. At the hour of eleven it was estimated that there were at least fifteen thousand persons assembled, and all things being in readiness, the marshals proceeded to form the line for the march.

THE ORDER OF MARCH

Alfred Kiger, chief marshal, wearing a yellow sash with pink trimmings, with William Shorter and William Nichols wearing blue sashes: mounted.

[Here follows a list of groups in the parade, from "United States colored troops" via "the Eastern Star Lodge," to the "Third Ward colored men." -ed.]

The procession moved in the above order, several policemen being in advance of to keep the way unobstructed.

Thousands of persons did not march in line, but thronged the sidewalks the entire length of the procession. Crowds had collected at the street corners along the route; and from many dwellings flags were displayed.

The multitude moved down I street, and as they passed General Howard's headquarters, at the corner of Nineteenth street, they cheered loudly. Thence on through I street to twentieth, down twentieth to F, and through F to Seventeenth, on the way cheering at the residence of Senator Pomery, who had flung an immense flag to the breeze. At the corner of Seventeenth and F streets cheers were given for Gen. Grant. Passing up Seventeenth street they cheered as they passed the War and Navy Departments, and when at Pennsylvania avenue turned to the right.

President Johnson, who, in spite of representing Tennessee in the Senate from 1857–1862 was strongly pro-Union, and was therefore selected by Lincoln to be military governor of Tennessee in 1862, then as his vice-president in 1864. Johnson became president on Lincoln's assassination.

A HALT AT THE EXECUTIVE MANSION

The fact being known that the procession would pass through the grounds of the Executive mansion, quite a throng had assembled in the grounds and about the portico, in the expectation that the president would probably make a speech. As the head of the procession defiled through the west gate of the enclosure of the Mansion, a salute was fired by a detail of the 4th United States Artillery, Captain Follet commanding. The colored troops were halted immediately in front of the portico, and in a twinkling, almost every available foot of ground was occupied, the crowd extending as far down as the gates on each side of the enclosure. Wile the military were being placed in position, President Johnson was notified by one of the marshals of the arrival of the procession, and he appeared at one of the upper windows, accompanied by Marshal Gooding, and was loudly cheered. The band then played "Hail Columbia;" and, in the meantime, the President, escorted by Marshal Gooding and Colonel W. G. Moore, his private secretary, came out of the main entrance of the Executive Mansion, and took his stand upon the stone coping under the front of the portico, and, after the cheers had subsided, he addressed the assembled multitude as follows:

SPEECH OF THE PRESIDENT

I have nothing more to say to you on this occasion that to thank you for this compliment you have paid in presenting yourselves before me on this your day of celebration. I come forward for the purpose of indicating my approbation and manifesting my appreciation of the respect thus offered and or conferred.

I thank you for the compliment and I mean what I say—and I will remark in this connection, that the time will come, and that too before a great while, when the colored population of the United States will find out who have selected them as a hobby and a pretense by which they can be successful in obtaining and maintaining power, and who have been their truest friends and wanted them to participate in and enjoy the blessings of freedom.

The time will come when it will be known who contributed as much as any other man, and who, without being considered egotistical, I may say, contributed to more in procuring the great national guarantee of the abolition of Slavery in all the States, by the ratification of the amendment to the Constitution of the United States, giving a national guarantee that Slavery shall no longer be permitted to exist or be reestablished in the jurisdiction of the United States.

I know how easy it is to cater to prejudice, and how easy it is to excite feelings of prejudices and unkindness. I care not for that. I have been engaged in this work, in which my life has been periled. I was not engaged in it as a hobby, nor did I ride the colored man for the sake of gaining power. What I did was for the purpose of establishing the great principle of freedom; and, thank God, I feel and know it to be so, that my efforts have contributed as much, if not more, than those of any other living man in the United States [Enthusiastic applause.] It is very easy for colored men to have pretend friends ensconced in high places, and far removed from danger, whose eyes have only abstractly gazed on freedom, who have never exposed their limbs of property, and who never contributed a sixpence in furtherance of the great cause, while another periled his all and put everything sacred and dear to man, and those whom he raised, and who lived with him, now enjoy his property, with his consent, and receive his aid and assistance. Yet some assume to be, and others who have done nothing are considered, the great defenders and protectors of the colored man. I repeat, my colored friends here to-day, the time will come, and that not far distant, when it will be proved who is practically your best friends. My friendship as far as it has gone, has not been for place or power, for I had these already. It has been a principle with me, and I thank God the great principle has been established that whenever any individual, in the language of

These words, often repeated by Frederick Douglass, were originally spoken in

1772 by John Philpott Curran, in arguing that James Somerset, a slave from Virginia, had been freed by being brought to England.

a distinguished orator, treads American soil, "his soul swells within him, in appreciation of the great truth that he stands forth redeemed, regenerated and disenthralled by the genius of universal emancipation." [Applause.] Then let me mingle with you in celebration of the day which commenced your freedom. I do it in sincerity and truth, and trust in God the blessings which have been conferred may be appreciated and enjoyed by you, and that you may give them a proper direction. There is something for all to do. You have high and solemn duties to perform, and you ought to remember that freedom is not a mere idea. It must be reduced to practical reality. Men in being free have to deny themselves many things which seem to be embraced in the idea of universal freedom. It is with you to give evidence to the world and the people of the United States whether you are going to appreciate this great boon as it should be, and that you are worthy of being freemen. Then let me thank you with the sincerity of the compliment you have paid me by passing through here to-day and paying your respects to me. I repeat again, that the time will come when you will know who have been your best friends, and who have not been your friends from mercenary considerations. Accept my thanks.

INCIDENTS AT THE EXECUTIVE MANSION

As soon as the President had concluded his remarks, an [sic -ed.] hundred black hands were extended toward him, and he complacently commenced a hand-shaking operation, which was no doubt very gratifying to those whose hands were shaken, but very trying to the President, who, from the position he occupied, was compelled to stoop over to grasp the hands extended to him. Marshal Gooding, with characteristic thoughtfulness, placed a chair for the President, and he sat down, but continued the hand shaking, which lasted about five minutes, the procession meanwhile filing by, each delegation cheering the Chief Magistrate as it passed, which salutation the President acknowledged, the hand shaking having been temporarily concluded. The rest of the procession having filed past, another rush was made for the President's hand, and hundreds more were gratified. One old colored woman, after heartily shaking the President's hand, uttered, with great solemnity, the words, "Live forever, glorious king!" This second greeting having terminated, the President re-entered the Executive Mansion.

FORWARD, MARCH!

Meanwhile the procession had moved along Pennsylvania avenue to Fifteenth street, down Fifteenth street to Pennsylvania avenue again, and thence to the Capitol, cheering the House of Representatives and the Senate Chamber. Passing entirely around the Capitol, the procession reappeared on Pennsylvania avenue on First street, and proceeded to Four-and-a-half street, up Four-and-a-half street to Indiana avenue, cheering at Speaker Colfax's resident and at the City Hall, along Indiana avenue to Fifth street, up Fifth to F, along F to Thirteenth, cheering at Senator Sumner's residence, and up Thirteenth street to Franklin Square, where an immense crowd had assembled.

THE COLORED SCHOOLS

The colored schools of the city did not assemble in front of the Executive Mansion, as was at first arranged, many of them being at too great a distance from that point fot the smaller children to walk there. It was afterwards decided that those schools east of Seventh street should assemble in front of the White House, on Pennsylvania avenue, the right resting on Seventeenth street.

At this point were collected the John Wesleyan College day school, numbering about one hundred scholars, headed by a banner bearing the inscription "Philadelphia Schools, The Mind the Master," and Wesley Seminary Sunday School, numbering about forty pupils.

Many of the larger male scholars took part in the procession, and no particular order seemed to be observed in the arrangement or stationing of the schools, they issued from their respective school rooms in excellent order, most of them under the care of colored female teachers, but the older boys soon became incorporated in the procession, while the teachers led their female flocks from point to point, as opportunities presented, to view the more attractive features of the procession.

Senator Charles Sumner (1811–1874) was Senator from Massachusetts from 1851 to 1874. He was a staunch abolitionist. He had been attacked on the Senate floor in 1856 after attacking Senators Douglas and Butler for their work writing the Kansas-Nebraska act.

THE MASS MEETING

Pending the arrival of the procession at Franklin Square, invited guests and the speakers had assembled upon the stand heretofore described. Among those present were Maj. Gen. O. O. Howard, Senators Wilson, Trumbull, Lane of Indiana, Howard, Chandler, Clark, Brig. Gen. Elkin, Brig. Gen Eaton, Bishop Parne, Rev. H. H. Garnett, Wm. Howard Day, &c., &c.

The meeting was called to order at half-past two o'clock by the chairman, George F. Cook, who introduced Bishop Payne, who offered a fervent prayer.

Mr. Cook then stated that he had letters from a number of distinguished gentlemen regretting their inability to be present, but as it was growing late he would not read the letters, but simply announce the names of the writers as follows: Senator Sumner, Hon. J. F. Wilson of Iowa, Rear Admiral C. H. Davis, Senators Sprague, Foster, and Norton, Speaker Colfax, Hon. W. D. Kelley, and Rev. Byron Sunderland. Each name as announced was greeted with applause, Messrs. Sumner, Kelley, and Colfax coming in for the largest share.

The chairman then introduced

REV. H. H. GARNETT

Henry Highland Garnett (1815–1882) was a Presbyterian minister, newspaper editor and abolitionist. He was born a slave in Kent County, MD, but escaped to New York City when he was 10. He was best known for his calls to slaves to live free or die.

who commenced by offering his congratulations upon the return of the anniversary of the day that brought freedom to the Capital of the nation. [Applause.] He presumed it was no longer a presumption in him to address the colored people as fellow-citizens since the Constitution had been amended so as to prohibit slavery, and since the civil rights bill has become the law of the land. [Applause.] To-day the principles if liberty are triumphant; the principles for which became a martyr, and which John Quincy Adams, Henry Winter Davis, Owen Lovejoy, Solomon Foot, and others uttered with their latest breath. Equal justice cannot be withheld from a portion of the American people if the Senate of the United States continues to be under the control of patriotic men who stand as a wall fire against any encroachment upon radical human rights. [Applause.] Nor need the colored men fear so long as the Supreme Court is filled with just judges, who believe that all men have rights, [Applause.] Look at the Senate of the United States. There stands the Senator from Massachusetts, with his feet firmly planted on the rock of ages, demanding justice for all. [Applause.] There, too, is Trumbull, the author of the Freedmen's Bureau bill, and although it failed in its passage, he was successful, for right is always successful. And there, too, is Wade, and Wilson, and Fessenden, and Nye, and the twenty-seven others forming a galaxy of light and ability. [Applause.] In the House of Representatives stands a veteran statesman, sagacious, dipped in the fire of living truth; and where Thaddeus Stevens [applause,] is, there justice lives and moves and has a being. There, too, are Kelley, and Wilson, and Colfax, and Grinnell, and the glorious one hundred and forty-one who are battling for our country's honor, and thank God! John W. Forney still lives to raise his voice and wield his pen for the rights of all men. [Applause.] The history of the last two hundred and eighty years shows that the black man cannot be blotted out. Like a cork, he may sink for awhile, but he will eventually rise to the surface. [Applause.] One year ago to-day Abraham Lincoln was lying in his coffin and a nation was weeping over his bier. The colored people were among the mourners, and were he living to-day he would smile upon their efforts. The speaker concluded by paying a tribute to the memory of Mr. Lincoln, and then proposed a preamble and resolutions commencing with a recommendation of the overruling power of Providence, and ascribing to God thanks and praise for the wonderful work done in this nation in causing the yoke of slavery to be broken.

2d. Recognizing the suffering and self-devotion and patience of the philanthropists of past years in the cause of liberty.

3d. Referring to the course of President Lincoln and declaring that in years to come, all who would participate in the joys of freedom would perpetuate his memory in grateful hears.

4th. Tendering heartfelt thanks to the Senators and Representatives in Congress who framed the laws abolishing slavery and securing civil rights to all, and pledging to them and to the country their loyalty and devotion, in peace and war.

5th. Is complimentary to the commanders of the army and navy of the United States, refers to the services of the colored soldier, and declares that it is the duty of a great people to remove all distinctions on account of color.

6th. Declares that the brave soldiers who, in time of war, perilled [sic -ed.] their lives, cannot have withheld from them the right of equal suffrage without wrong and injustice, and declaring that in this work, Congress would begin in the American Jerusalem, which is the District of Columbia. [Applause.]

7th. Recognises [sic -ed.] the important services of the Freedmen's Bureau in behalf of the colored people, and declares that, without its aid, emancipation would be such only in name.

8th. Expresses sympathy with all persons seeking equal rights, and especially with the colored people of Jamaica, Brazil, and Cuba.

9th. Declares that the freedmen's idea of equal rights, and of liberty, is the privilege of earning his bread by the sweat of his brow, of doing a fair day's labor for an equivalent, and of faithfully discharging his duty to his country, his family, and his God.

10th Declares that the colored people are sensible of the fact that they are engaged in a stubborn war, with unrelenting foes of prejudice, but are determined to fight it out; and their weapons will be the spelling-book, the Bible, and industrial pursuits, and their watchword loyalty to their God and country.

The resolutions were adopted by acclamation.

HON. LYMAN TRUMBULL

Senator from Illinois, was next introduced as the author of the

Senator Trumbull (1813–1896,

Senator from 1855–1873) was one of President Johnson's chief antagonists. Absolutely anti-slavery, Trumbull co-authored the 13th Amendment. He also worked against the so-called Black Codes, which were passed in the late 1860's and were early forerunners of the Jim Crow laws of the late 19th Century.
In spite of this, Trumbull voted for acquittal during Johnson's impeachment. He —and all other Republicans who voted against acquittal—was not re-elected.

On August 6, 1861, Lincoln signed the first confiscation act, which stated that any slave taking up arms against the Union would be considered free.

civil rights bill, and his appearance was greeted with applause. He addressed the multitude as his fellow-citizens, which caused renewed applause, and said he had come to rejoice with them in this anniversary of their freedom—a freedom from the most abject bondage that ever existed—a freedom that made each of them as much of a freeman as he was himself; that prevented a father from being torn from his children and a mother from her infant. This great boon was now secured to the colored race, but it had not been secured without a struggle. It had taken time and had not been accomplished by mere human instrumentality. The credit for the freedom enjoyed by four million of citizens belonged to Omnipotence, and some of us were but the instruments used to bring about the greatest and grandest of all results. The first step in the great plan of emancipation was taken at the special session of Congress convened by Mr. Lincoln in 1861, when, in July of that year, a bill was introduced, which became a law in August following, discharging from servitude all who were claimed as slaves, and who were made use of in aid of the rebellion, [applause,] and all who then claimed slaves were rebels. [Applause.] That was the beginning of emancipation. In 1862 was passed the act which made free the slaves of the District of Columbia. [Applause.] You meet to celebrate the fourth anniversary of that act. Then, however, freedom was made on compensation, and one million of dollars was appropriated t pay men who had no more right to your service than you had to theirs. But we have learned better since then. [Laughter and applause.] On the 17th of July, 1862, was passed the first great act of emancipation—an act which proclaimed that all who were held as slaves, who fled and came in sight of the country's flag, should be free. [Applause.] The President of the United States, in September, 1862, promulgated that law in a proclamation, and called the attention of the commanders of our army and navy to its enforcement; and he said if the rebels would not return to their allegiance at a specified time, all slaves should be declared free. When that time arrived, January 1, 1863, he declared slavery abolished in nine of the States and a portion of two others, leaving four of the States and portions of two others untouched. The Congress of the United States, at a subsequent day, in February, 1863, determined a foundation as immutable as Government itself. [Applause.] And they engrafted an amendment upon the Constitution, declaring that slavery or involuntary servitude should not exist in the land, except as a punishment for crime. [Renewed applause.] That amendment has been ratified since this Congress assembled, and it is now one of the pillars on which the Government stands. The great amendment extended to all the land, and it will extend over the whole continent when it is all embraced in the United States. [Applause.] However, this great declaration was not all that was necessary. It mattered little to you to be free if you could not enjoy that freedom. The declaration of Independence said all men are created equal, yet you derived no benefit from it. Some means were required for your protection, so that when your rights were encroached upon you should have in your hands the means to vindicate those rights. [Applause.]

That law was passed Monday one week ago. [Applause.] It is a part and parcel of the great constitutional amendment, and is intended to give it practical effect. It declares that every man, no matter what color, is an American citizen; and it will be as valuable to you to protect you as in ancient days, when a man could protect himself from wrong and injustice by simply declaring, "I am a Roman citizen." [Applause.]e great rights, which the Great Author of us all gave to all men, have now been restored to you, and it is now for you to show that you are worthy of American citizenship, and that would be done the speaker said he had no doubt. The colored people were now as free as he (the speaker) was, and it is for you to prove yourselves worthy and entitled to the high privileges you enjoy, and the spirit of freedom inaugurated here will spread throughout the world, and the time will come when no man will look another in the face and call him master. [Applause.]

In conclusion, the speaker said that legislation had done all it could to secure to the negro life, liberty, and property, and the rest depended on themselves. Henceforth it will be impossible to make any law which will discriminate in favor of a class; and under the operation of the civil rights bill, if a law is passed to deprive the negro of a right, it will also deprive the white man of that right. [Applause.] Equality before the law belongs to the negro from this time henceforth, and, by the blessings of God, the speaker hoped forever. [Applause.]

HON. HENRY WILSON

Senator from Massachusetts, was next introduced, and was received with applause. He said that as he gazed to-day upon this mighty throng in the capital of his country; as he gazed on the banners fluttering in the breeze; as he listened to the music of the band, his thoughts turned back one-third of a century ago to that little assembly of God-fearing men who laid the foundation we now enjoy. [Applause.] He remembered that when they met together, and ten States were represented, they decided to do all for the abolition of slavery. [Applause.] The work was begun one-third of a century ago by a body of humble but devoted men, and

For more information on Senator Wilson, see page 53.

it has gone on from struggle to struggle, and to-day not a slave treads the soil of the continent from the Delaware to the Rio Grande. [Applause.] Not a wide can be torn from her husband; not a child from its parent, and not a bloodhound can bay on the track of a slave. Thank God, through the labors of a few men all fetters are broken, and each colored man can say for himself, I am a man and a brother, and a citizen of the North American Republic. [Applause.] The speaker said he well remembered how bills for the overthrow of slavery were received in the Senate of the United States. He remembered how the bill introduced by Mr. Trumbull in July, 1861, was received, when the traitor Breckinridge, sitting in the Senate with a heart full of treason, said he saw in that bill the loosing of all bonds. Yes, it *was* the loosing of all bonds, and we have gone on from that little measure until we have passed the civil rights bill. [Applause.]

The speaker was going on to speak of the civil rights bill when

THE STAGING FELL

and dignified Senators, brave soldiers, busy reporters, white and colored citizens were unceremoniously precipitated to the ground, and found a common level. Senator Wilson, who was standing upon a chair, was precipitated backward with much force, and it was at first feared that he had received injury, but he subsequently turned up all right. Two or three chairs and a bench were broken; coats were torn and hats were crushed. Senator Trumbull lost his hat, and had not succeeded in finding it for half an hour after the accident had occurred. Two ladies were upon the stand, but they sustained no injury other than a badly mutilated parasol. Some boys had been playing under the staging, and it was at first feared that a life or lives had been lost; but upon removing the boards no such fatal result was found, much to the gratification of all present.

The multitude then moved to the music stand, and the speaking continued there.

SENATOR WILSON

was applauded upon his reappearance, and said he had come back again. During the last thirty years they had sometimes bad falls, but they always rose again. [Laughter.] The friends of human freedom are sometimes baffled, checked, and temporarily defeated, but they always rise again bolder than before. The great civil rights bill, though a great measure, was not the only measure for the security of the negro. On war the bullet had been put in the hands of the black man, and he was asked to defend the country, and in the hour of victory, as sure as God lives, the American people will yet put the ballot in his hands, so as to protect and preserve the unity and prosperity of the Republic. [Applause.] In this their hour of rejoicing, the speaker said he wanted them to resolve and proclaim that they demanded the rights of American citizens, and meant to make themselves worthy. Their race had for eight generations toiled and worked in this western world. They had toiled with unrequited toil, and were here now and could not be sent out of the country. [Applause.] The Blairs may utter their gibberish about sending out four millions and a half of toiling men, and others may repeat their words, but the needs of a people will keep them here as a part of the American people and citizens of the great republic of the Western World. [Applause.] You are to be here to have the rights we have, and to enjoy the blessings we enjoy; and let us labor by night and by day to lift up the lowly and pull no one down. God made the world large enough for his children. Our country is large enough, and we want all good me to stay here; and we know that the blacks are worthy to be a portion of the North American Republic. [Applause.] The speaker said that he learned that the President told them to-day that they would soon find out who were their friends. As the President claims to be the colored man's friend, he [the speaker] would say that they did not wish to dispute his claim. He is *our* president, put where he is by the votes of anti-slavery men, and put there to exercise his high office on the side of justice and right. Let him be the colored man's friend. He [the speaker] wished to God that in all his acts and words the President would place himself as much in advance of others, as the friend of the negro, as he is elevated above them, [the Senators.] We ask the President to go forward, and instead of disputing with him who is the negro's best friend, we will hail him as their best friend when he proves himself such. [Applause.]

MAJOR GENERAL O. O. HOWARD

was the next speaker, and he said it gave him more than ordinary pleasure to participate in such an occasion as this. He was grateful to the black soldiers,as well as to the white ones, for what they had done; but he ascribed the glory to Almighty God. The speaker proceeded to argue that love was the bond and fundamental law, and the very bottom of reconstruction. We are required to love God and love humanity. It is not *like*; it is *love*, with all its depth of meaning. It requires a little more if the spirit of Christ to make our people agree and make us a homogeneous people. We need to make the proud man weak, so that he will learn to love all men. When a youth, the speaker said, he learned the Scripture text,

The brothers Francis P. Blair, Jr. (Representative from Missouri 1857–1864 and General in the Union Army) and Montgomery Blair (who was postmaster-general in Lincoln's cabinet) were both Republicans and firm believers in the forced emigration of freed slaves.

Oliver Otis Howard (1830–1909) spent his entire career in the army, including the whole Civil War, in which he fought in both the battles of Chancellorsville and Gettysburg. Howard was instrumental in founding Howard University, which bears his name.

"Love the Lord thy God with all thy heart, and they neighbor as thyself;" but he had not learned that the black man was excluded. The speaker continued to argue upon the necessity of love to all men, and said he wanted every man and woman to combat every doctrine and put down every party until we shall have practical acknowledgment of universal liberty. The colored people have now a glorious law, and it is like the Magna Charta, the charter of their rights. [Applause.] When it became a law it lifted, the speaker said, a heavy load from his heart, because he was identified with the interest of the freedmen, and he felt that the law was necessary to make freedom more than the mere name. He would acknowledge no right in other men that was denied to the black man. That had always been his principle, and he would adjure his hearers to stand firmly by truth and justice. The speaker conclude by invoking the blessing of God upon Congress, and to keep them steadfast, and also upon the President and his counsellors, [sic -ed.] and trusted and hoped that they might be united with Congress on the basis of liberty, law, right, truth, and love.

WILLIAM HOWARD DAY

William Howard Day (1825–1900) was a clergyman, editor, and abolitionist. At this time, he was working for the freedmen's bureau, where he helped found schools.

a colored orator from New York was next introduced, and made a speech which was received with much applause. In the course of his remarks he said they were celebrating one of the grandest events in the history, not only of this country, but in that of the world. Emancipation of the colored race was not the result of accident, but a part of the grand purpose of the Almighty. Justice to the colored race had not been realized all at once, but had come step by step, and there was more to be done, for they had not been accorded all justice yet. It tends to a yet higher point, and that is, suffrage for all. [Applause.] Emancipation was the natural results of the true principles of the American Government. Slavery was always a traitor in the Government. When Massachusetts, Pennsylvania, Rhode Island, New Hampshire, and New Jersey successively abolished slavery, the slave power raved, and it has been mad ever since. The slave power held that if slavery could be maintained in the District of Columbia it could be maintained everywhere. We took their line of argument and said, begin to abolish slavery in the District of Columbia, and abolition will spread everywhere. [Applause.] The speeches referred to the fact that in 1828 an effort was made for gradual emancipation in this District, at the request of its own citizens, and argued that at that time most European governments were in favor of doing away with the crime, and that but for its existence here it would have been abolished. Referring to the argument that the extension of the right of suffrage to colored me would be fraught with more evil than good, the speaker combated it by saying that the negroes of New York now owned property valued at $2,500,00, whereas before they possessed the right of suffrage they held but little property. The fact that so much opposition to granting the negro the ballot shows that slavery is not dead, and that negroes need the ballot to kill it. The speaker concluded by reading a poem of his own composition.

A resolution was adopted tendering the thanks of the meeting to Secretary Harlan for granting the use of Franklin Square, and to Secretary Stanton, Lieutenant General Grant, and General Augur, for favors shown.

A vote of thanks was then also tendered to each of the speakers and the chairman then announced that a collection would be taken up to defray the expenses, and the meeting then adjourned.

The very best order prevailed throughout the entire day and the whole celebration was in all respects creditable to the colored people of this District. The principal movers in the affair were old and well-known residents of the District, and they manifested a pride to have all things conducted decently and in order. They have reason to be gratified at the success of their effort.

James Harlan (1820–1899) was Secretary of the Interior in President Johnson's cabinet.

William H. Day and O. O. Howard.

Picture of Day taken from print *Distinguished Colored Men.* Published in New York by A. Muller & Co. c1883.
Picture of Howard from *The Nez Percés War from Sketches by an Army Officer.* published in *Harper's Weekly,* October 27, 1877. (both from Library of Congress)

The Emancipation statue in Lincoln Park shortly after its erection. The Library of Congress lists the picture as being from 1870, which is obviously impossible. The picture is taken towards the southeast. Two major changes have been made to the statue in the meantime: A plaque was added to the base, and the statues themselves were turned to face the statue of Mary Macleod Bethune that was erected at the east end of the park. 'Freedom's Memorial' plaque was placed on the east side some time between 1876 and 1918. This plaque is now on the west side. The other plaque, installation date unknown, has the inscription:

"And upon this Act sincerely believed to be an act of justice warranted by the constitution upon military necessity I invoke the considerable judgement of mankind and the gracious favor of almighty God.
A. Lincoln Emancipation Proclamation Jany 1, 1863
Western Sanitary Commission
James E Yeatman President.
C. S. Greeley Treas:
Geo. Partridge. Dr. J. B. Johnson.
Wm. C. Eliot."

Two members of Lincoln's cabinet were similarly honored by having Squares in Capitol Hill named after them: William Henry Seward's name graces the area at the confluence of Pennsylvania and North Carolina Avenues, while Edward Stanton's named has been given to the intersection of Massachusetts and Maryland Avenues. (from Library of Congress)

Oration by Frederick Douglass

Delivered in Lincoln Park
April 14, 1876

> The emancipation celebration in 1876 was combined
> with the unveiling of a statue commemorating Lincoln's
> emancipation of the slaves. The unveiling was held on
> the 11th anniversary of Lincoln's assassination. His
> speech was preceded by a reading of the Emancipation
> Proclamation, the actual unveiling, as well as a
> recitation of the eighty-line poem "Today, O martyred
> chief, beneath the sun" by Cornelia Ray.

Friends and Fellow-Citizens:

I warmly congratulate you upon the highly interesting object
which has caused you to assemble in such numbers and spirit as
you have today. This occasion is in some respects remarkable.
Wise and thoughtful men of our race, who shall come after us,
and study the lesson of our history in the United States; who shall
survey the long and dreary spaces over which we have traveled;
who shall count the links in the great chain of events by which we
have reached our present position, will make a note of this
occasion; they will think of it and speak of it with a sense of
manly pride and complacency.

I congratulate you, also, upon the very favorable circumstances in which we meet today. They are high, inspiring, and
uncommon. They lend grace, glory, and significance to the object
for which we have met. Nowhere else in this great country, with
its uncounted towns and cities, unlimited wealth, and im-
measurable territory extending from sea to sea, could conditions
be found more favorable to the success of this occasion than here.

We stand today at the national center to perform something
like a national act—an act which is to go into history; and we are
here where every pulsation of the national heart can be heard, felt,

The 'interest-
ing object' had
been subject
of bitter dis-
cussions in its
creation. The
final appear-
ance is, to
modern eyes,
quite conde-
scending—and
was consid-
ered thus back
when it was
built. Though
Douglass here
refrains from
directly criti-
cizing the
monument, he
had not been
nearly as reti-
cent earlier.

and reciprocated. A thousand wires, fed with thought and winged with lightning, put us in instantaneous communication with the loyal and true men all over the country.

Few facts could better illustrate the vast and wonderful change which has taken place in our condition as a people than the fact of our assembling here for the purpose we have today. Harmless, beautiful, proper, and praiseworthy as this demonstration is, I cannot forget that no such demonstration would have been tolerated here twenty years ago. The spirit of slavery and barbarism, which still lingers to blight and destroy in some dark and distant parts of our country, would have made our assembling here the signal and excuse for opening upon us all the flood-gates of wrath and violence. That we are here in peace today is a compliment and a credit to American civilization, and a prophecy of still greater national enlightenment and progress in the future. I refer to the past not in malice, for this is no day for malice; but simply to place more distinctly in front the gratifying and glorious change which has come both to our white fellow-citizens and ourselves, and to congratulate all upon the contrast between now and then; the new dispensation of freedom with its thousand blessings to both races, and the old dispensation of slavery with its ten thousand evils to both races—white and black. In view, then, of the past, the present, and the future, with the long and dark history of our bondage behind us, and with liberty, progress, and enlightenment before us, I again congratulate you upon this auspicious day and hour.

Friends and fellow-citizens, the story of our presence here is soon and easily told. We are here in the District of Columbia, here in the city of Washington, the most luminous point of American territory; a city recently transformed and made beautiful in its body and in its spirit; we are here in the place where the ablest and best men of the country are sent to devise the policy, enact the laws, and shape the destiny of the Republic; we are here, with the stately pillars and majestic dome of the Capitol of the nation looking down upon us; we are here, with the broad earth freshly adorned with the foliage and flowers of spring for our church, and all races, colors, and conditions of men for our congregation—in a word, we are here to express, as best we may, by appropriate forms and ceremonies, our grateful sense of the vast, high, and preeminent services rendered to ourselves, to our race, to our country, and to the whole world by Abraham Lincoln.

The sentiment that brings us here today is one of the noblest that can stir and thrill the human heart. It has crowned and made glorious the high places of all civilized nations with the grandest and most enduring works of art, designed to illustrate the charac-

Though Douglass seems to think that the anti-Black feelings are relegated to 'dark and distant parts of our country' the end of reconstruction, and the concomitant rise of violence against ex-slaves was begun later in 1876, with the election of Rutherford Hayes.

ters and perpetuate the memories of great public men. It is the sentiment which from year to year adorns with fragrant and beautiful flowers the graves of our loyal, brave, and patriotic soldiers who fell in defense of the Union and liberty. It is the sentiment of gratitude and appreciation, which often, in the presence of many who hear me, has filled yonder heights of Arlington with the eloquence of eulogy and the sublime enthusiasm of poetry and song; a sentiment which can never die while the Republic lives.

For the first time in the history of our people, and in the history of the whole American people, we join in this high worship, and march conspicuously in the line of this time-honored custom. First things are always interesting, and this is one of our first things. It is the first time that, in this form and manner, we have sought to do honor to an American great man, however deserving and illustrious. I commend the fact to notice; let it be told in every part of the Republic; let men of all parties and opinions hear it; let those who despise us, not less than those who respect us, know that now and here, in the spirit of liberty, loyalty, and gratitude, let it be known everywhere, and by everybody who takes an interest in human progress and in the amelioration of the condition of mankind, that, in the presence and with the approval of the members of the American House of Representatives, reflecting the general sentiment of the country; that in the presence of that august body, the American Senate, representing the highest intelligence and the calmest judgment of the country; in the presence of the Supreme Court and Chief-Justice of the United States, to whose decisions we all patriotically bow; in the presence and under the steady eye of the honored and trusted Cabinet, we, the colored people, newly emancipated and rejoicing in our blood-bought freedom, near the close of the first century in the life of this Republic, have now and here unveiled, set apart, and dedicated a figure of which the men of this generation may read, and those of after-coming generations may read, something of the exalted character and great works of Abraham Lincoln, the first martyr President of the United States.

Douglass fails to mention the most important person attending the ceremony: President Ulysses S. Grant, who also actually unveiled the statue.

Fellow-citizens, in what we have said and done today, and in what we may say and do hereafter, we disclaim everything like arrogance and assumption. We claim for ourselves no superior devotion to the character, history, and memory of the illustrious name whose monument we have here dedicated today. We fully comprehend the relation of Abraham Lincoln both to ourselves and to the white people of the United States. Truth is proper and beautiful at all times and in all places, and it is never more proper and beautiful in any case than when speaking of a great public man whose example is likely to be commended for honor and imitation long after his departure to the solemn shades, the silent continents of eternity. It must be admitted, truth compels me to admit, even here in the presence of the monument we have erected to his memory, Abraham Lincoln was not, in the fullest sense of the word, either our man or our model. In his interests, in his associations, in his habits of thought, and in his prejudices, he was a white man.

He was preeminently the white man's President, entirely devoted to the welfare of white men. He was ready and willing at any time during the first years of his administration to deny, postpone, and sacrifice the rights of humanity in the colored people to promote the welfare of the white people of this country. In all his education and feeling he was an American of the Americans. He came into the Presidential chair upon one principle alone, namely, opposition to the extension of slavery. His arguments in furtherance of this policy had their motive and mainspring in his patriotic devotion to the interests of his own race. To protect, defend, and perpetuate slavery in the states where it existed Abraham Lincoln was not less ready than any other President to draw the sword of the nation. He was ready to execute all the supposed guarantees of the United States Constitution in favor of the slave system anywhere inside the slave states. He was willing to pursue, recapture, and send back the fugitive slave to his master, and to suppress a slave rising for liberty, though his guilty master were already in arms against the Government. The race to which we belong were not the special objects of his consideration. Knowing this, I concede to you, my white fellow-citizens, a pre-eminence in this worship at once full and supreme. First, midst, and last, you and yours were the objects of his deepest affection and his most earnest solicitude. You are the children of Abraham Lincoln. We are at best only his step-children; children by adoption, children by forces of circumstances and necessity. To you it especially belongs to sound his praises, to preserve and perpetuate his memory, to multiply his statues, to hang his pictures high upon your walls, and commend his example, for to you he was a great and glorious friend and benefactor. Instead of supplanting you at his altar, we would exhort you to build high his monuments; let them be of the most costly material, of the most cunning workmanship; let their forms be symmetrical, beautiful, and perfect, let their bases be upon solid rocks, and their summits lean against the unchanging blue, overhanging sky, and let them endure forever! But while in the abundance of your wealth, and in the fullness of your just and patriotic devotion, you do all this, we entreat you to despise not the humble offering we this day unveil to view; for while

Douglass professed a different view of Lincoln's attitudes later in his life, writing in his essay "Lincoln and the Colored Troops:" "In all my interviews with Mr. Lincoln I was impressed with his entire freedom from popular prejudice against the colored race. He was the first great man that I talked with in the United States freely, who in no single instance reminded me of the difference between himself and myself, of the difference of color, and I thought that all the more remarkable because he came from a State where there were black laws." Allen T. Rice,

Abraham Lincoln saved for you a country, he delivered us from a bondage, according to Jefferson, one hour of which was worse than ages of the oppression your fathers rose in rebellion to oppose.

Fellow-citizens, ours is no new-born zeal and devotion—merely a thing of this moment. The name of Abraham Lincoln was near and dear to our hearts in the darkest and most perilous hours of the Republic. We were no more ashamed of him when shrouded in clouds of darkness, of doubt, and defeat than when we saw him crowned with victory, honor, and glory. Our faith in him was often taxed and strained to the uttermost, but it never failed. When he tarried long in the mountain; when he strangely told us that we were the cause of the war; when he still more strangely told us that we were to leave the land in which we were born; when he refused to employ our arms in defense of the Union; when, after accepting our services as colored soldiers, he refused to retaliate our murder and torture as colored prisoners; when he told us he would save the Union if he could with slavery; when he revoked the Proclamation of Emancipation of General Fremont; when he refused to remove the popular commander of the Army of the Potomac, in the days of its inaction and defeat, who was more zealous in his efforts to protect slavery than to suppress rebellion; when we saw all this, and more, we were at times grieved, stunned, and greatly bewildered; but our hearts believed while they ached and bled. Nor was this, even at that time, a blind and unreasoning superstition. Despite the mist and haze that surrounded him; despite the tumult, the hurry, and confusion of the hour, we were able to take a comprehensive view of Abraham Lincoln, and to make reasonable allowance for the circumstances of his position. We saw him, measured him, and estimated him; not by stray utterances to injudicious and tedious delegations, who often tried his patience; not by isolated facts torn from their connection; not by any partial and imperfect glimpses, caught at inopportune moments; but by a broad survey, in the light of the stern logic of great events, and in view of that divinity which shapes our ends, rough hew them how we will, we came to the conclusion that the hour and the man of our redemption had somehow met in the person of Abraham Lincoln. It mattered little to us what language he might employ on special occasions; it mattered little to us, when we fully knew him, whether he was swift or slow in his movements; it was enough for us that Abraham Lincoln was at the head of a great movement, and was in living and earnest sympathy with that movement, which, in the nature of things, must go on until slavery should be utterly and forever abolished in the United States.

Reminiscences of Abraham Lincoln by Distinguished Men of His Time. New York: Harper & Brother, Publishers, 1885.

When, therefore, it shall be asked what we have to do with the memory of Abraham Lincoln, or what Abraham Lincoln had to do with us, the answer is ready, full, and complete. Though he loved Caesar less than Rome, though the Union was more to him than our freedom or our future, under his wise and beneficent rule we saw ourselves gradually lifted from the depths of slavery to the heights of liberty and manhood; under his wise and beneficent rule, and by measures approved and vigorously pressed by him, we saw that the handwriting of ages, in the form of prejudice and proscription, was rapidly fading away from the face of our whole country; under his rule, and in due time, about as soon after all as the country could tolerate the strange spectacle, we saw our brave sons and brothers laying off the rags of bondage, and being clothed all over in the blue uniforms of the soldiers of the United States; under his rule we saw two hundred thousand of our dark and dusky people responding to the call of Abraham Lincoln, and with muskets on their shoulders, and eagles on their buttons, timing their high footsteps to liberty and union under the national flag; under his rule we saw the independence of the black republic of Haiti, the special object of slave-holding aversion and horror, fully recognized, and her minister, a colored gentleman, duly received here in the city of Washington; under his rule we saw the internal slave-trade, which so long disgraced the nation, abolished, and slavery abolished in the District of Columbia; under his rule we saw for the first time the law enforced against the foreign slave trade, and the first slave-trader hanged like any other pirate or murderer; under his rule, assisted by the greatest captain of our age, and his inspiration, we saw the Confederate States, based upon the idea that our race must be slaves, and slaves forever, battered to pieces and scattered to the four winds; under his rule, and in the fullness of time, we saw Abraham Lincoln, after giving the slave-holders three months' grace in which to save their hateful slave system, penning the immortal paper, which, though special in its language, was general in its principles and effect, making slavery forever impossible in the United States. Though we waited long, we saw all this and more.

Can any colored man, or any white man friendly to the freedom of all men, ever forget the night which followed the first day of January, 1863, when the world was to see if Abraham Lincoln would prove to be as good as his word? I shall never forget that memorable night, when in a distant city I waited and watched at a public meeting, with three thousand others not less anxious than myself, for the word of deliverance which we have heard read today. Nor shall I ever forget the outburst of joy and thanksgiving that rent the air when the lightning brought to us the emancipation

Captain Nathaniel Gordon (1826–1862) was the only person ever convicted of slave trading. He was captured in 1861, shortly after taking on almost 900 slaves in West Africa, was tried twice, convicted the second time and sentenced to hang. After a two-week stay of execution was approved by Lincoln, he was hung on February 21, 1862.

proclamation. In that happy hour we forgot all delay, and forgot all tardiness, forgot that the President had bribed the rebels to lay down their arms by a promise to withhold the bolt which would smite the slave-system with destruction; and we were thenceforward willing to allow the President all the latitude of time, phraseology, and every honorable device that statesmanship might require for the achievement of a great and beneficent measure of liberty and progress.

Fellow-citizens, there is little necessity on this occasion to speak at length and critically of this great and good man, and of his high mission in the world. That ground has been fully occupied and completely covered both here and elsewhere. The whole field of fact and fancy has been gleaned and garnered. Any man can say things that are true of Abraham Lincoln, but no man can say anything that is new of Abraham Lincoln. His personal traits and public acts are better known to the American people than are those of any other man of his age. He was a mystery to no man who saw him and heard him. Though high in position, the humblest could approach him and feel at home in his presence. Though deep, he was transparent; though strong, he was gentle; though decided and pronounce in his convictions, he was tolerant towards those who differed from him, and patient under reproaches. Even those who only knew him through his public utterance obtained a tolerably clear idea of his character and personality. The image of the man went out with his words, and those who read them knew him.

I have said that President Lincoln was a white man, and shared the prejudices common to his countrymen towards the colored race. Looking back to his times and to the condition of his country, we are compelled to admit that this unfriendly feeling on his part may be safely set down as one element of his wonderful success in organizing the loyal American people for the tremendous conflict before them, and bringing them safely through that conflict. His great mission was to accomplish two things: first, to save his country from dismemberment and ruin; and, second, to free his country from the great crime of slavery. To do one or the other, or both, he must have the earnest sympathy and the powerful cooperation of his loyal fellow-countrymen. Without this primary and essential condition to success his efforts must have been vain and utterly fruitless. Had he put the abolition of slavery before the salvation of the Union, he would have inevitably driven from him a powerful class of the American people and rendered resistance to rebellion impossible. Viewed from the genuine abolition ground, Mr. Lincoln seemed tardy, cold, dull, and indifferent; but measuring him by the sentiment of his country, a sentiment he was bound as a statesman to consult, he was swift, zealous, radical, and determined.

Though Mr. Lincoln shared the prejudices of his white fellow-countrymen against the Negro, it is hardly necessary to say that in his heart of hearts he loathed and hated slavery. The man who could say, "Fondly do we hope, fervently do we pray, that this mighty scourge of war shall soon pass away, yet if God wills it continue till all the wealth piled by two hundred years of bondage shall have been wasted, and each drop of blood drawn by the lash shall have been paid for by one drawn by the sword, the judgments of the Lord are true and righteous altogether," gives all needed proof of his feeling on the subject of slavery. He was willing, while the South was loyal, that it should have its pound of flesh, because he thought that it was so nominated in the bond; but farther than this no earthly power could make him go.

This is a close paraphrase of a section of Lincoln's Second Inaugural Address. See, for example, Josiah G. Holland. The Life of Abraham Lincoln. Springfield, Mass.: Gurdon Bill, 1866. p. 504.

Fellow-citizens, whatever else in this world may be partial, unjust, and uncertain, time, time! is impartial, just, and certain in its action. In the realm of mind, as well as in the realm of matter, it is a great worker, and often works wonders. The honest and comprehensive statesman, clearly discerning the needs of his country, and earnestly endeavoring to do his whole duty, though covered and blistered with reproaches, may safely leave his course to the silent judgment of time. Few great public men have ever been the victims of fiercer denunciation than Abraham Lincoln was during his administration. He was often wounded in the house of his friends. Reproaches came thick and fast upon him from within and from without, and from opposite quarters. He was assailed by Abolitionists; he was assailed by slave-holders; he was assailed by the men who were for peace at any price; he was assailed by those who were for a more vigorous prosecution of the war; he was assailed for not making the war an abolition war; and he was bitterly assailed for making the war an abolition war.

But now behold the change: the judgment of the present hour is, that taking him for all in all, measuring the tremendous magnitude of the work before him, considering the necessary means to ends, and surveying the end from the beginning, infinite wisdom has seldom sent any man into the world better fitted for his mission than Abraham Lincoln. His birth, his training, and his natural endowments, both mental and physical, were strongly in his favor. Born and reared among the lowly, a stranger to wealth and luxury, compelled to grapple single-handed with the flintiest hardships of life, from tender youth to sturdy manhood, he grew strong in the manly and heroic qualities demanded by the great mission to which he was called by the votes of his countrymen.

The hard condition of his early life, which would have depressed and broken down weaker men, only gave greater life, vigor, and buoyancy to the heroic spirit of Abraham Lincoln. He was ready for any kind and any quality of work. What other young men dreaded in the shape of toil, he took hold of with the utmost cheerfulness.

> "A spade, a rake, a hoe,
> A pick-axe, or a bill;
> A hook to reap, a scythe to mow,
> A flail, or what you will."

These are the first four lines of Thomas Hood's poem, "The Lay of the Labourer" Hood (1799–1845) was a British poet and humorist.

All day long he could split heavy rails in the woods, and half the night long he could study his English Grammar by the uncertain flare and glare of the light made by a pine-knot. He was at home in the land with his axe, with his maul, with gluts, and his wedges; and he was equally at home on water, with his oars, with his poles, with his planks, and with his boat-hooks. And whether in his flat-boat on the Mississippi River, or at the fireside of his frontier cabin, he was a man of work. A son of toil himself, he was linked in brotherly sympathy with the sons of toil in every loyal part of the Republic. This very fact gave him tremendous power with the American people, and materially contributed not only to selecting him to the Presidency, but in sustaining his administration of the Government.

Upon his inauguration as President of the United States, an office, even when assumed under the most favorable condition, fitted to tax and strain the largest abilities, Abraham Lincoln was met by a tremendous crisis. He was called upon not merely to administer the Government, but to decide, in the face of terrible odds, the fate of the Republic.

A formidable rebellion rose in his path before him; the Union was already practically dissolved; his country was torn and rent asunder at the center. Hostile armies were already organized against the Republic, armed with the munitions of war which the Republic had provided for its own defense. The tremendous question for him to decide was whether his country should survive the crisis and flourish, or be dismembered and perish. His predecessor in office had already decided the question in favor of national dismemberment, by denying to it the right of self-defense and self-preservation—a right which belongs to the meanest insect.

Happily for the country, happily for you and for me, the judgment of James Buchanan, the patrician, was not the judgment of Abraham Lincoln, the plebeian. He brought his strong common sense, sharpened in the school of adversity, to bear upon the question. He did not hesitate, he did not doubt, he did not falter; but at once resolved that at whatever peril, at whatever cost, the union of the States should be preserved. A patriot himself, his faith was strong and unwavering in the patriotism of his country-men. Timid men said before Mr. Lincoln's inauguration, that we have seen the last President of the United States. A voice in in-fluential quarters said, "Let the Union slide." Some said that a Union maintained by the sword was worthless. Others said a re-bellion of 8,000,000 cannot be suppressed; but in the midst of all this tumult and timidity, and against all this, Abraham Lincoln was clear in his duty, and had an oath in heaven. He calmly and bravely heard the voice of doubt and fear all around him; but he had an oath in heaven, and there was not power enough on earth to make this honest boatman, backwoodsman, and broad-handed splitter of rails evade or violate that sacred oath. He had not been schooled in the ethics of slavery; his plain life had favored his love of truth. He had not been taught that treason and perjury were the proof of honor and honesty. His moral training was against his saying one thing when he meant another. The trust that Abraham Lincoln had in himself and in the people was surprising and grand, but it was also enlightened and well founded. He knew the American people better than they knew themselves, and his truth was based upon this knowledge.

The voice saying "Let the Union slide" was that of Nathaniel P. Banks, Representative from Massachusetts and later Major-General in the Union army. While others were willing to accommodate slavery in the United States, Banks insisted that he would rather let the Union slide. He spoke these words at a rally in Portland, Maine, in 1855.

Fellow-citizens, the fourteenth day of April, 1865, of which this is the eleventh anniversary, is now and will ever remain a memorable day in the annals of this Republic. It was on the evening of this day, while a fierce and sanguinary rebellion was in the last stages of its desolating power; while its armies were broken and scattered before the invincible armies of Grant and Sherman; while a great nation, torn and rent by war, was already beginning to raise to the skies loud anthems of joy at the dawn of peace, it was startled, amazed, and overwhelmed by the crowning crime of slavery—the assassination of Abraham Lincoln. It was a new crime, a pure act of malice. No purpose of the rebellion was to be served by it. It was the simple gratification of a hell-black spirit of revenge. But it has done good after all. It has filled the country with a deeper abhorrence of slavery and a deeper love for the great liberator.

Had Abraham Lincoln died from any of the numerous ills to which flesh is heir; had he reached that good old age of which his vigorous constitution and his temperate habits gave promise; had he been permitted to see the end of his great work; had the solemn curtain of death come down but gradually—we should still have been smitten with a heavy grief, and treasured his name lovingly.

But dying as he did die, by the red hand of violence, killed, assassinated, taken off without warning, not because of personal hate—for no man who knew Abraham Lincoln could hate him—but because of his fidelity to union and liberty, he is doubly dear to us, and his memory will be precious forever.

Fellow-citizens, I end, as I began, with congratulations. We have done a good work for our race today. In doing honor to the memory of our friend and liberator, we have been doing highest honors to ourselves and those who come after us; we have been fastening ourselves to a name and fame imperishable and immortal; we have also been defending ourselves from a blighting scandal. When now it shall be said that the colored man is soulless, that he has no appreciation of benefits or benefactors; when the foul reproach of ingratitude is hurled at us, and it is attempted to scourge us beyond the range of human brotherhood, we may calmly point to the monument we have this day erected to the memory of Abraham Lincoln.

Frederick Douglass a few years after his speech. Detail of print *Distinguished Colored Men.* Published in New York by A. Muller & Co. c1883. (from Library of Congress)

EMANCIPATION DAY.

[Read by Milton Holland at the Emancipation Banquet, Washington, D. C., April 13th, 1883.]

Sound aloud the trump of freedom,
Let the answering echo ring,
While with liberty commanding,
We our heartfelt tribute bring;
As we gather round Columbia,
Let us scatter on the way
Flowers of love and flowers of trusting,
For Emancipation Day.
Let us pray for benedictions
While we bow in reverence low
At the shrine of noble heroes,
Bravely charging on the foe.
Gladly we hear our welcome,
To this feast of Liberty.

WELCOME.

Lo, the car of progress moving,
Over all Columbia's land;
Gifted men are proudly coming
And we take them by the hand—
Men of different race and color,
Yet our peers in soul and brain,
And their names shall soon be sculptured
On the towering dome of fame.

Emancipation Day

Poem by Mary E. Kail
April 13, 1883

As time passed, Emancipation Day events became more organized and elaborate. They included, for instance, an Emancipation Banquet that was part of the 21st anniversary celebration.

In honor of this event, Mrs Mary E. Kail, a noted patriotic poet of the time, wrote a poem entitled "Emancipation Day." Mrs Kail, who hailed from Ohio, was a staunch Republican, and was working at the time as an auditor in the Treasury Department, a job she was given in return for the campaign songs she had written for the Republican party.

Mrs. Kail lost her job when Democrat Grover Cleveland won the 1884 election, and no attempts to sway the Secretary of the Treasury to reverse his decision had any affect. After Cleveland's defeat in 1888, Kail returned to DC and resumed her job, dying there on January 28, 1890.

Illustration on opposite page is page 51 of Mary Kail, *Crown our Heroes and Other Poems*, Judd & Detweiler, Washington DC, 1887, showing the first lines of the poem Mary Kail wrote in honor of this celebration, (From Google Books)

EMANCIPATION DAY

Sound aloud the trump of freedom,
Let the answering echo ring,
While with liberty commanding,
We our heartfelt tribute bring;
As we gather round Columbia,
Let us scatter on the way
Flowers of love and flowers of trusting,
For Emancipation Day.
Let us pray for benedictions
While we bow in reverence low

125

At the shrine of noble heroes,
Bravely charging on the foe.
Gladly we hear our welcome,
To this feast of Liberty.
        WELCOME.
Lo, the car of progress moving,
Over all Columbia's land;
Gifted men are proudly coming
And we take them by the hand—
Men of different race and color,
Yet our peers in soul and brain,
And their names shall soon be sculptured
On the towering dome of fame.

Float aloft the stars of glory,
For we love to tell the story
That is written on the pages
Of Columbia's record true;
How amid the cannon's rattle,
And the shot and shell of battle,
Chains of living death were broken
By our gallant boys in blue!

Ah! our soldiers never faltered;
Never heeded they the gloom;
Quailed not when the shock of battle
Seemed the eternal knell of doom;
But with comrades pale and bleeding
Only heard Columbia pleading—
"Wipe away from my escutcheon
Every trace of human woe.
Let my rightful sons and daughters
Of whatever race they be,
Hear the clarion voice of heroes,
Making way for liberty.

Let no cloud of dark oppression
Linger in Columbia's sky;
Let the joyful shout of freedom
Rise aloft to God on high!"

Days were dark and fierce the struggle—
Can it be the day is lost?
Came from many an anguished mother,
As she reckoned up the cost
Of the blood and of the treasure,
Given freely without measure,
As the price of liberty.

But amid the desolation.
Spreading o'er our glorious-land
Came the news—Emancipation
Has been reached—the proclamation,
Far above the cannon's roar
Sounded loud, o'er hill and valley
Bells were ringing, hearts were singing,
As they never sung before.

For the shackels had been broken,
And four million souls were free,
That 'till then had never tasted
Of the joys of liberty!
And to-day we gladly greet them,
As we gather 'round to meet them,
And to take them by the hand—
Men whose throbbing souls ignited
At the watch-fires freedom lighted.
Freedom's altar fires, still burning
Flash and sparkle at each turning,
As the car of progress moving,
Rolls them on to nobler fame.

W. C. CHASE.

Print of William Calvin Chase taken from William J. Simmons. *Men of Mark: Eminent, Progressive and Rising.* Cleveland: Geo. M. Rewell & Co., 1887. (from Harvard College Library via Google Books)

Emancipation Day

The Evening Star
April 14, 1883

The 1883 celebrations had enough material for the *Evening Star* to give up portions of three newspapers to describe it: The preparations and plans were detailed on April 14, the march was written up the day it happened —April 16—while that evening's program was written up only the next day.

Since plan and implementation were pretty much one and the same, the article from the 14th, giving a sense of the thought that went into the celebration, is reprinted below.

Emancipation Day
THE PREPARATIONS FOR THE CELEBRATION NEXT MONDAY—THE ORDER OF PROCESSION AND PROGRAM OF THE EVENING CEREMONIES.

Judging from present indications the twenty-first anniversary of the emancipation of slaves in the District of Columbia will be celebrated here on Monday in a manner which will do credit to the race, and with an *éclat* surpassing all former celebrations of the event. For several weeks the chief marshal, Mr. P. H. Carson, the members of the various committees, the master of ceremonies, Mr. M. M. Holland, and others have been engaged in the work of preparation. Last evening the several committees, at a meeting at the Philadelphia House, made reports indicating the perfection of every detail. During the day there will be a monster procession.

THE EVENING CEREMONIES.

At night the main celebration will be at the Congregational Church, when the exercises will be as follows:

Music, Cornet Band; prayer, Rev. J. E. Rankin; reading letters of regret and resolution, W. C. Chase, secretary of the committee on speakers; address, Milton M. Holland, master of ceremonies; address, orator of the evening, Hon. Fred. Douglass; music, Cornet Band; address, Rev. R. S. Laws; music, Cornet Band; address, Col. Robert G. Ingersoll; music, Cornet Band; benediction, Rev. J. E. Rankin.

This portion of the celebration is in charge of the following committee of arrangements: John W. Freeman, chairman; C. C. Brisco, secretary; George W. Stewart, W. H. Black, A. St. A. Smith, G. W. Robinson, C. C. Stewart, James Garner, George H. Boston, Wm. Talliafero, W. C. Chase, R. W. Laws, Charles Marshall, W. K. Brown.

AN EAST WASHINGTON CELEBRATION.

The associations in East Washington will have an evening celebration at the Enon Baptist Church, when Rev. C. W. Walker, of Baltimore, will deliver an address.

Milton M. Holland (1844–1910) was a Civil War hero from Texas. He received the medal of honor in 1865 for bravery displayed during the Battle of Chapin's Farm, Sept. 29, 1864. He is buried in Arlington Cemetery.

AN ADDRESS TO THE PUBLIC.

The following address to the citizens of the District was issued:

To the Citizens of the District of Columbia.

The approaching anniversary of the abolition of slavery in this District will be celebrated with becoming ceremonies, and to make the occasion one worthy of the memories, and to make the occasion one worthy of the memories that clusters around it, is a duty devolving on all who would perpetuate the love of human dignity.

The day can be made one of which none of us will be ashamed if the worth and intelligence of the community will give their hearty support to those who have engaged to carry out the program already arranged; and knowing as we do the public-spiritedness of our citizens, and their readiness to magnify the doctrines of human freedom on all proper occasions, we confidently ask for your presence and active participation in the exercises of the day.

Come together, then, on the anniversary of the day that brought liberty to the bondman at the national capital, and make it one every way worthy of the glorious past, in keeping with the progressiveness of the present, and suggestive of the widening future.

April 14, 1883   MILTON M. HOLLAND
                                  President of the Day.

THE PROCESSION

will be formed under Chief Marshal P. H. Carson Monday morning, on New Jersey avenue, the right resting on Indiana avenue. After the formation of the procession the line of march will be taken up at 11 o'clock, passing up Indiana avenue, by Lincoln statue, down 4½ street past the Columbia building, where the military and civic procession will be reviewed by the District Commissioners; down Pennsylvania avenue to the north side of the Capitol; east Capitol to 6th street east; down 6th street to Pennsylvania avenue; down Pennsylvania to the south side of the capitol on B street; thence to 4½ street; thence to Pennsylvania avenue; up Pennsylvania, passing in review by the President's House to Georgetown; round the water fountain to M street; thence east to Connecticut avenue; out Connecticut avenue to K street; down K to 3d street; down 3d to Indiana avenue; then to south side of City Hall, where the procession will disband.

The Lincoln Statue mentioned is today located on Judiciary Square, and was sculpted by Lot Flannery and placed there April 15, 1868, the third anniversary of Lincoln's death. There are six total Lincoln statues in public places in the District of Columbia; this was the first erected.

The military part of the procession will include the Langston guards, of Norfolk, VA.; the Monumental Rifles, of Baltimore, and also companies from Richmond and Petersburg, besides our local military, as follows:

Butler Zouaves, 52 in number, commanded by Major B. Fisher; Capital City Guards, A company, 48 muskets, commanded by Capt. T. S. Kelly; company B, Capital City Guards, 46 muskets, commanded by Capt. Gray; Washington Cadets, 62 muskets, Capt. Fleetwood; Lincoln Light Infantry, 37 muskets, Capt. Tucker, and a company of horse artillery, to act in conjunction with Major Hanneman, of the District artillery, mounted, but without guns, under Capt. Ralph Wormley.

There will also be in line the Knights of Jerusalem, Josephus Commandery, No. 1 Galileean Fishermen, Knights of Moses, Knights of St. Augustine, the Friends of Zion, Chaldeans, Knights of Labor, Knights Templar, Hod Carrier's Union, Brickmakers' Union, the Osceola, Sold Yantic, Monitor, Celestial Golden Link, Lively Eight, Imperial Independent Fern Leaf, Arthur Social, Invincible, Costometic, Ethiopian Gay Heart Domico Clubs, Eastern Star and Twilight Cadets.

There will be several six-horse cars, finely decorated in various colors, on which will be enthroned respectively the Queen of Freedom, the Goddess of Liberty and other imaginary deities. These cars will be interspersed in the civic portion of the procession, and will form an interesting feature of the occasion. There will be several original mottoes and designs introduced in the line.

NOTES.

At the meeting of the committees on finance and arrangements, at the Philadelphia house last evening, the committee of arrangements reported that final arrangements had been made, and that the procession would be the largest one that has ever been seen in the District of Columbia. Mr. W. C. Chase, from the sub-committee on arrangements and secretary of the committee on speakers, reported that the departments had granted leave of absence to the colored employes. [sic -ed.] A congratulatory letter was read from Mr. A. M. Clapp, and a vote of thanks for services rendered was tendered to Mr. Lewis H. Douglas.

The Baltimore Rifles, with the Monumental Cornet Band, and the Monumental City Guards and Excelsior Brass Band will arrive from Baltimore, via B. & P. railroad, at 9:30 o'clock Monday morning. The Rifles will be received by company A, Capital City Guard, and the Monumental City Guards by the Butler Zouaves.

MILTON M. HOLLAND.

Picture of Milton Holland from Lewis Wallace *et al. The Story of American Heroism: Thrilling Narratives of Personal Adventures During the Great Civil War*, Springfield, Ohio: J. W. Jones, 1897.
(From New York Public Library via Google Books)

Their Day of Freedom

The Washington Post
April 17, 1897

Towards the close of the 19th Century, Emancipation Day celebrations in DC became increasingly fraught. Although as late as 1899, President McKinley still reviewed the parades, internal dissension about how the celebrations were to be run, as well as public disapproval thereof, took its toll. One year, 1886, there were even two parades. The principal agitator against the parades that year—and for many years—was William Calvin Chase, editor of the *Washington Bee*.

The following article gives a sense of the Emancipation Day celebrations in their decline, the internal dissensions, and the general low regard in which they were held by the white citizens of the country.

THEIR DAY OF FREEDOM

Emancipation Parade Reviewed by the President.

ADDRESSES AT LINCOLN PARK

Calvin Chase Argues Against Parades as a Feature of the Celebrations—Should Present Evidence of the Negro's Progress—Great Enthusiasm at the White House and Along the Line of March—The Organization in the Procession.

This article appeared in *The Washington Post* of April 17, 1897

District Emancipation Day dawned bright and clear yesterday morning and the colored man of Washington breathed a sigh of relief as he donned his blue sash and pinned the large rosette upon the left breast of his coat, under which the heart of a freeman beat to a quicker time at the idea that he would be allowed to march through the streets of the Capital City in celebration of the grand act of a martyred President.

The arrangements were for a parade and an open-air meeting, where from a platform in the park named after the man whose act was celebrated, the orators might pronounce eulogies and mark the epochs in words that blazed with patriotism.

The arrangements were all satisfactory and the carrying them out caused but few delays and hitches. The arrangements were that the parade should start at noon, but it was some time after 2 when it moved.

The procession was to form in the neighborhood of Dupont Circle. Colored people began to gather in this vicinity about 11 o'clock, and by 12 there were several hundred standing on the cub. After an hour had passed the spectators began to think that they had been misinformed about the the location where the parade was to form, when the Manhattan Pioneers No. 4 were seen approaching, and and a flutter of excitement was noticeable among the colored maidens gathered there. The Pioneers carried fierce-looking wooden battle-axes, but their warlike appearance was offset by yachting caps perched jauntily on their heads. The Young Eagle Drum Corps then hove into sight, leading the Butler Zouaves. After this the different companies, organizations, and individuals began to arrive. The parade was long and varied, and after the ranks had been formed the order to march was given about 2 o'clock and the parade was in motion.

Order of Procession.

List of groups in the parade, from a platoon of mounted police to the Third division, "consisting of a chariot, a ship, and carriages, containing the officers of the various clubs" excised.

The official order was as follows:

...

Listened to Stirring Speeches.

There were several halts and hitches after the parade started, and it was a few minutes past 3 when it reached the White House. The grounds were filled with colored people, and they raised a mighty shout when President McKinley stepped upon the portico to review the parade. The enthusiasm of the spectators was shared by those composing the procession, and they loudly cheered the President as they passed.

The parade then passed down Pennsylvania avenue and was greeted by large crowds, who cheered lustily all along the line of march. It turned into Louisiana avenue at Seventh street, and was reviewed by Commissioners Ross and Black from a window in the District Building. It then proceeded to Lincoln Park, where a platform had been erected and a number of addresses were made.

The opening address was by George W. Stewart, the President of the day. W. Calvin Chase was the orator of the day. Magnus L. Robinson, of Virginia, read the Emancipation Proclamation, and then there were addresses by Prof. Jesse Lawson, E. M. Hewlett, Richard Laws, and others. Mr. Chase's oration was greeted with great applause. He spoke with much feeling, and the majority of his audience appeared in sympathy with him.

"Our freedom is made a mockery of by street parades," said Mr. Chase. "They show up the disgraceful side of the negro: he is presented as he was, and not as he is, in some instances. Instead of a street parade, the President of the United States should have been asked to witness some productions of our public school children.

"What evidence has the President to-day that the negro in the District of Columbia has produced anything since his emancipation? Did we present anything in our parade to-day to make an impression of any power? It is always the custom to present the greatest objects that will tend to impress. Instead of having the beating of drums and blowing of horns there should have been shown evidences of our progress since emancipation."

M. L. ROBINSON.

E. M. HEWLETT.
Harvard Graduate. U. S. Magistrate D.C.

On the left, a drawing of Magnus L. Robinson from Irvine Garland Penn, *The Afro-American Press and Its Editors*, Springfield MA, Willey & Co,1891. Robinson was the editor of the *Washington National Leader*. (From the Stanford Library via Google Books)

On the right, drawing of E. M. Hewlett, from J. J. Pipkin, *The Story of a Rising Race*. N. D. Thompson Publishing Company, 1902. Hewlett was Frederick Douglass's son's brother-in-law. (from Google Books)

The Colored American

A NATIONAL NEGRO NEWSPAPER

VOL. IX, NO. 51   WASHINGTON, D. C., APRIL 18, 1903.   PRICE, FIVE CENTS

The Premier Ministrel

"The Smart Set," a Theatrical Aggregation of Colored Talent.

Messrs. Ernest Hogan and Billy Mc-Clain Capture the Nation's Capital. The Plot of the Play and the Growth of Colored Thespians.—The personnel of the Troup.

The Smart Set, the theatrical aggregation on which Ernest Hogan and Billy McClain are the ruling stars has been with us. They left an impression for good as it concerns the colored people's capacity and aptitude for all lines of theatrical work. In many respects the show was a notable departure from the exhibitions of the past, in that it sought to put a better front to Negro life, surrounding it with just enough of comedianism and burlesque, as to make an excellent background, or setting for the whole.

Ernest Hogan in the minds of many cannot be supplanted the premier comedianship lies between about three people, and Hogan has strong supporters for the place. In his peculiar line he can scarcely be excelled. He is evidently a student of nature; his comicalities and witticisms are the result of art so perfect, that it appears the individual. One would suspect Mr. Hogan to act on the streets precisely as he does on the stage, so near to nature is he. His power lies in his gestures, what he implies as much so as in what he says; he is a great comedian. He is also a philosopher as was proven by his dying request to his wife, "tell her to stay off of Indiana avenue."

Billy McClain makes good support for Mr. Hogan. He makes a clever villain and sport, the roles he assumes. Of course the audience is not entrapped with the character as is always noted. He acted his part well however, giving evidence of dramatic ability. Miss Margaret Jordan is a very pleasing singer with a graceful figure. Her prima donna work deserves much praise. Her movement, voice and fig. ure caught the audience. H. Jackson Norris is a man of superb figure. His singing was a feature of the show. He has not many more pleasing singers than Mr. Jackson. To say he sings grandly expresses it.

Men of the Hour

Mr. Ernest Hogan,
New York's Premier Comedian and Song Writer Now with the Smart Set Company

The singing of the Dinwiddie Quartette, was an acceptable feature, the voices were well modulated, sweet and harmonious.

The work of Marion Henry with Hogan was a clever bit of acting. Hogan thought she looked "good," there were others. She is blessed with a prepossessing figure, good voice, grace and dignity, the essentials for a successful stage career. She also knew how to put on her clothes, and she had them to put on. Ben Bunn's singing of "Gable," was a great hit with the audience.

Mosama, the much sought for, was all right when she did put in her appearance. What little plot there is hinges on this Kentucky darling that has strayed away to the Hawaiians. Much of the finer work of the show is based on the habits of the islanders as they are supposed to be. The Roosevelt Lodge skit is about as clever as anything seen on the stage. The initiation is something fierce, the oldest

lodge man has never seen anything like it; it will certainly do.

The ensemble singing all along was good, much of which was operatic in effect and in the personnel the coon songs were good, but not so numerous as in similar shows of the past. The costuming was superb.

Taking it all in all there was but very little chance for adverse criticism.—The Freeman.

What do you think of the new dress of The Colored American? For verily, Solomon in all his glory approached not to this magnificence.

Admirers of Bishop Williams and they are legion, take off their hats to Editor Cooper for the magnificent tribute of last week. The colored photograph issued as a supplement represents the highest development of pictorial art, and a handsome man has received worthily a handsome compliment.

FORTY YEARS OF FREEDOM.

For the American Negro Hindrance and Progress

Rev. C. T. Walker, D. D., of New York, Pastor of Mt. Olivet Baptist Church, and Gotham's Most Eloquent and Learned Divine, Tells of His Race and Its Marvelous Progress and Achievements.—Facts and Figures.

The first day of January, 1863, the immortal Abraham Lincoln signed the Emancipation Proclamation, liberating more than four million human slaves, who had been held in cruel bondage nearly 250 years. The signing of the Proclamation was the central act of his administration, and the greatest event of the 19th century. The history of my race is very similar to that of the Jewish nation.

The Jews were enslaved in Egypt for a period of 400 years, and endured great persecution under cruel taskmasters. It was the Providence of God that they should come in touch with Egyptian civilization, receive the necessary training and discipline to become a great nation, produce great leaders, statesmen, poets, Kings, Judges, prophets and scholars; and give a code of laws to the world. The Jew was carried from Canaan to Africa to be enslaved. The Negro was brought from Africa to America and enslaved.

God overthrew Egyptian slavery after sending ten plagues upon the Egyptian slave-holders; and overthrew American slavery by the plague of war, which lasted four years.

The Israelites numbered about three millions at the time of their emancipation; the American Negroes numbered four millions at the time of their liberation. The Jews returned to the land of their nativity by way of the Red Sea, passing Sinai to get laws, statutes and ordinances, camping in the wilderness forty years to receive discipline and training.

The Negro remained in the land that had been the theatre of his enslavement, and humiliation, and for forty years has been sailing upon the Red Sea, of trouble, persecution, discrimination, murder, lynching, burnings, mob rule, injustices, and disfranchisements.

The Negro as a slave deserved great credit for the Spirit of love and kindness he exhibited toward his former master. His loyalty and devotion during four years of the most cruel war in the annals of history is without a parallel. He guarded, defended and supported defenseless women, and helpless children, while the master fought to tighten his chains. He kissed the hand that smote him; and wept over the dead body of his master, as sincerely as Jacob mourned for Joseph. While many northern states

Continued on page 4.

Emancipation's Travail and Triumph

John R. Wennersten

W hat happened to all the lofty dreams of equality and civic participation after the Civil War engendered by racial emancipation in the District and the South generally? Simply put, the United States Congress and the American people lost their nerve. Immediately after the war Congress passed a series of Reconstruction Acts to rehabilitate and federalize the late rebellious states. Under this legislation, Blacks in the South and in the District achieved a measure of political power, which was mostly directed towards the resettlement, and education of the freedmen. The 14th and 15th Amendments to the Constitution gave emancipation and civil rights to the African-American the kind of federal force that would be beyond the whims of any president or backward leaning Congress.

During the late 19th century Blacks in the District voted and attended schools. Congress established Howard University, a Black federally funded university in the District that continues to carry the name of a white union general, Oliver O. Howard, the director of the Freedmen's Bureau. For many years the Federal government, pushed by liberal northern opinion, showed willingness and a determination to intervene to protect the rights of Black Americans.

Until the late 1890s, Black optimism in cities in the south was reflected in "emancipation parades," large, entertaining spectacles usually taking place in April in the District and at various other times, most notably on June 19 ("Juneteenth") in Galveston, Texas. These parades also served as a reflection of Black social and economic achievement and were a measure of Black progress in the community.

Northern support of the African American began to dissipate in the 1870s when it became clear that federal protection of Blacks in the face of determined white racist opposition would require massive appropriations of federal funds and the use of a standing army of occupation in the South to maintain order against racial terrorist organizations like the Ku Klux Klan. Emancipation's bright star began to dim when President Rutherford B. Hayes pulled all the federal troops out of the south after 1877.

As many scholars of the period between 1877 and 1900 have noted, without federal intervention, Southern states established racially repressive regimes based on violence. Even in areas where Blacks were an absolute majority such as Louisiana, Mississippi, and South Carolina, racist whites overturned free and fair elections and used the Klansmen and other "nightrider groups" to suppress the African American community.

A system of racial segregation and control emerged in the South known as Jim Crow. Blacks could not attend the same schools as whites. Blacks were prevented from voting and could not ride next to whites on trains and streetcars. Blacks walked in the gutter while white man and women strode the sidewalks. While social conditions in the District were better for the African American in the post-Emancipation era, Blacks still experienced their share of reprisals and sanctions as they sought to rise in society. For example, it was not until Frederick Douglass bought a large home formerly owned by a white in Anacostia that Blacks in the 1880s could acquire property outside of the community of tenements and Black housing developments like Barry Farm. Meanwhile many Blacks left the south and settled in Washington and northern cities where opportunities were neither as miserable nor as marginal as they were in Dixie. It is interesting to note that when the United States Supreme Court gutted the 14th and 15th Amendments and legalized Jim Crow in the south under the dictum "Separate But Equal," in 1896, all the members on the Supreme bench were from the north.

Starting in the 1890s the national press began to carry a host of racial cartoons that caricatured African-Americans as stupid and shiftless folk who wanted nothing more than a federal hand out. The press also depicted Emancipation parades as licentious brawls known for drunkenness and fornication. The District's Black middle class worried that the Emancipation Parades would bring white disapproval down on their heads. "Is there anyway to stop these disgraceful Emancipation parades," argued the *Washington Colored American*. Black journalist W. Calvin Chase, editor of the *Washington Bee*, complained "these Emancipation Day Parades have fallen into the hands of sharks who do nothing but collect money from patriotic citizens and put it into their pockets." The Emancipation Day celebration had become an event, Chase fumed, to "support a set of lazy good for nothing

Washington Colored American, 18 April,1903. See p. 136

and idle shysters." The *Bee* and the *Colored American* both noted a serious decline in the moral and political fervor of the parades, which earlier had focused on speeches and public demonstrations about racism, lynching, and disfranchisement of blacks in the south. Also by the turn of the century, Emancipation celebrations had diminishing white patronage. The April 1899 Emancipation Day Parade was reviewed by President William McKinley and the District of Columbia City Commissioners. It was the last parade to enjoy such large bi-racial and presidential support. By 1902 colored ministers in the District openly discouraged "the custom of parades etc." Increasingly, the national press also began to portray blacks as unreliable citizens and members of what even staid organs like the *New York Times* referred to as the "dangerous class." Blacks fueled the racism of the white press by arguing that many emancipation speeches "would have had better effort on the inmates of St. Elizabeth (Lunatic) Asylum" than they would have in the District generally.

Emancipation as a celebratory event, however, occasionally showed a spark of political agitation. During the April 16, 1901 event, black orators at several mass meetings in the District met to protest the "betrayal of the hope and progress of the Negro." Specifically at this time black leaders in the city denounced disfranchisement of blacks in the south despite the 15th Amendment, Said one public petition to the Republican Party: "Time and again deputations of colored people visited Washington, DC and implored members of the Republican Party to mitigate the tyrannical mob law under which (Negroes) now suffer in most of the southern states." Some 500,000 immigrants poured into America in at the turn of the century, blacks protested, and they were generally treated far better than "loyal Negroes who would lay down their lives for the flag of this country." In what would be a final demonstration, the Lincoln Emancipation League marched from South Capitol Street to Lincoln Park to hear eulogies of Abraham Lincoln, John Brown and the abolitionists. Said one colored minister: "we have passed through one ordeal (slavery) – the next is coming."

In 1915 D.W. Griffith, produced his popular film, *Birth of A Nation* condemning Reconstruction in the South and portraying blacks as sexually obsessed savages. President Woodrow Wilson loved the film and termed it "history written in lightening." A southerner from Virginia and a foe of hiring blacks in the District offices of the federal government in Washington, Wilson wanted the rules of Jim Crow strictly enforced in the nation's capital.

In the words of the noted black scholar Rayford Logan, the African American had gone from emancipation to the "nadir." of

For more information on the "nadir" see Rayford Logan,

Betrayal of the Negro: from Rutherford B. Hayes to Woodrow Wilson, New York: Perseus Publishing. 1997.

national betrayal as harrowing as it was heartbreaking. One District black minister likened the Negro to the Israelites and their misfortunes. "We are sailing upon the Red Sea of trouble, persecution, murder, lynching, burning, mob rule and disfranchisement"

The troubled times of the post-Civil War era and the "nadir" of racial segregation in the nation's capital were part of a historical cycle that gradually gave way to racial amelioration and what Abraham Lincoln referred to in 1864 as "a new birth of freedom." Starting with the founding of the NAACP in the 1890s, civil rights for African-Americans was always part of the post-emancipation agenda. African-Americans in the decades before World War II protested against segregated facilities in Washington and the South generally. Throughout the 1930s and 1940s NAACP lawyers protested against the "separate but equal" *Plessy v. Ferguson* Supreme Court decision of 1896 which rendered racial segregation constitutional.

In Washington, on Capitol Hill before the United States Supreme Court, lawyers for the NAACP led by Thurgood Marshall, an attorney well-known in the District, won their case against segregation in America with the *Brown v. Board of Education* decision in 1954. And in 1964 President Lyndon Johnson signed the epic Civil Rights Act which set the nation on a steady course towards racial desegregation and an expanding climate of tolerance and equality before the law for African Americans.

Today in Washington, DC and elsewhere, African Americans have joined a middle class that continues to expand its diversity component. They have joined the chorus of "only in America uplift." African-Americans can proudly gaze upon the emancipation statues in Lincoln Park and contemplate one simple fact. The road to equality that began with the troubled early days of emancipation has now led to the White House in Washington, D.C. Barack Obama, a dedicated student of Abraham Lincoln and his legacy, is now the first African-American president of the United States.

District of Columbia Emancipation Day Amendment Act of 2004

Signed by DC Mayor Anthony Williams
January 4, 2005

DC Emancipation day was not the only emancipation celebration to go into decline at the beginning of the 20th century. As more slaves and their descendants moved to cities and away from farms, it became ever more difficult to organize Juneteenth celebrations, with the Great Depression, and the upheavals from World War II reducing their scope dramatically.

Starting in the 50s and 60s, however, efforts were made to restart these festivities, with a major push coming in 1968 with the Poor People's March on Washington. Finally, in 1980, Texas became the first state to make Juneteenth an official holiday. A number of states followed suit, and today 29 states (plus the District of Columbia) recognize June 19th as an official holiday.

Similarly, in the District of Columbia, efforts were made to restart emancipation celebrations. Here the date was fixed on April 16, and Mayor Anthony Williams signed legislation in 2004 making it an official holiday.

The legislation he signed is below.

AN ACT

IN THE COUNCIL OF THE DISTRICT OF COLUMBIA

To amend the District of Columbia Government Comprehensive Merit Personnel Act of 1978, to make April 16th, the District of Columbia Emancipation Day, a recognized legal public holiday.

BE IT ENACTED BY THE COUNCIL OF THE DISTRICT OF

COLUMBIA, That this act may be cited as the "District of Columbia Emancipation Day Amendment Act of 2004."

Sec. 2. The Council finds that:

(1) When President Lincoln signed An Act for the Release of certain Persons held to Service or Labor in the District of Columbia ("District of Columbia Emancipation Act") on April 16, 1862, freeing all slaves in the District, the law provided for immediate emancipation, compensation of up to $300 for each slave to loyal Unionist masters, voluntary colonization of former slaves to colonies outside the United States, and payments of up to $100 to each former slave choosing emigration. The federal government paid almost $1 million for the freedom of approximately 3,100 former slaves.

(2) It is important to the descendants of those free blacks and slaves, and to all other citizens in the District that this important moment in our country's and the District's history be formally recognized by the District.

(3) June 19, 1865 ("Juneteenth"), the day that the last slaves in the state of Texas were notified that President Lincoln had signed the Emancipation Proclamation on January 1, 1863, is celebrated annually in more than 205 cities and is a legal state holiday in Texas, Oklahoma, Florida, Delaware, and Iowa.

(4) In 1997, the United States Senate adopted a joint resolution recognizing Juneteenth as the true independence day for African-American citizens.

(5) The legal public holiday of the District of Columbia Emancipation Day would commemorate and celebrate April 16, 1862 as the day President Lincoln signed the District of Columbia Emancipation Act ending slavery in the District of Columbia, 9 months before the signing of the Emancipation Proclamation on January 1, 1863. The District of Columbia Emancipation Day will symbolize for Americans the triumph of the human spirit over the cruelty of slavery.

Sec. 3. Section 1202 of the District of Columbia Government Comprehensive Merit Personnel Act of 1978, effective March 3, 1979 (D.C. Law 2-139; D.C. Official Code §1-612.02(c)), is amended as follows:

(a) The existing text is designated as paragraph (1).

(b) A new paragraph (2) is added to read as follows:

"(2) April 16 of each year starting in 2005 shall be District of

Columbia Emancipation Day, which shall be a legal public holiday for the purpose of pay and leave of employees scheduled to work on that day; provided, that in 2005 and 2006, it shall be celebrated on the date of April 16 and not on the following Monday.".

Sec. 4. Sense of the Council.

It is the sense of the Council that the federal government should recognize the District of Columbia Emancipation Day. The Council urges Congresswoman Norton to introduce legislation in Congress to recognize this day.

Sec. 5. Fiscal impact statement.

The Council adopts the fiscal impact statement provided by the Chief Financial Officer as the fiscal impact statement required by section 602(c)(3) of the District of Columbia Home Rule Act, approved December 24, 1973 (87 Stat. 813; D.C. Code § 1-206.02(c)(3)).

Sec. 6. Effective date.

This act shall take effect following approval by the Mayor (or in the event of veto by the Mayor, action by the Council to override the veto), a 30-day period of Congressional review as provided in section 602(c)(1) of the District of Columbia Home Rule Act, approved, December 24, 1973 (87 Stat. 813; D.C. Official Code §1-206.02(c)(1)), and publication in the District of Columbia Register.

Chairman

Council of the District of Columbia

Mayor

District of Columbia

Addendum

March 14, 1862.— LETTER TO J. A. McDOUGALL.

EXECUTIVE MANSION, WASHINGTON, March 14, 1862.

HON. JAMES A. McDOUGALL, United States Senate.

My dear Sir: As to the expensiveness of the plan of gradual emancipation with compensation, proposed in the late message, please allow me one or two brief suggestions.

Less than one half day's cost of this war would pay for all the slaves in Delaware at four hundred dollars per head.

Thus, all the slaves in Delaware by the census
of 1860, are   1,798
                                                400

Cost of the slaves $719,200
One day's cost of the war 2,000,000

Again, less than eighty-seven days' cost of this war would, at the same price, pay for all in Delaware, Maryland, District of Columbia, Kentucky, and Missouri.

Thus, slaves in Delaware   1,798
  "   "   Maryland   87,188
  "   "   District of Columbia   3,181
  "   "   Kentucky   225,490
  "   "   Missouri   114,965

                                              432,622
                                                  400

Cost of slaves $173,048,800
Eighty-seven days' cost of the war 174,000,000

Do you doubt that taking the initiatory steps on the part of those States and this District would shorten the war more than eighty-seven days, and thus be an actual saving of expense?

A word as to the time and manner of incurring the expense. Suppose, for instance, a State devises and adopts a system by which the institution absolutely ceases therein by a named day— say January 1, 1882. Then let the sum to be paid to such a State by the United States be ascertained by taking from the census of 1860 the number of slaves within the State, and multiplying that number by four hundred — the United States to pay such sums to the State in twenty equal annual instalments, in six per cent. bonds of the United States.

The sum thus given, as to time and manner, I think, would not be half as onerous as would be an equal sum raised now for the indefinite prosecution of the war; but of this you can judge as well as I. I inclose a census table for your convenience.

Yours very truly,   A. LINCOLN.

Letter from Abraham Lincoln to James McDougall, describing the cost of compensated emancipation vs. cost of the war. Page impression from John G. Nicolay and John Hay, eds., *Abraham Lincoln Complete Works, Volume 2.* New York: The Century Co., 1894. (from Stanford University library via Google Books)

Lincoln's first inauguration with unfinished Capitol Dome in background. Photograph by Benjamin French. (from Library of Congress)

"President Lincoln's Reinauguration at the Capitol, March 4, 1865. Photographed by [Alexander] Gardner, Washington." Print from *Harper's Weekly*, March 18, 1865 (from sonofthesouth.net)

FRIENDS OF SOUTHEAST LIBRARY

403 7th St. SE, Washington, DC 20003

This book is published by Friends of Southeast Library, a 501(c)(3) organization of volunteers, established in 1982 to encourage local use and support for the D.C. Public Library and its southeast neighborhood branch, to encourage reading, and to promote the history and culture of Capitol Hill. This project was supported in part by a grant from the Humanities Council of Washington, D.C.